Edinburgh

Edinburgh University Press

paPerbacks

A.A.PARKER

Literature and the Delinquent

A classic study in the sociology of literature. It traces the changing concept of the 'picaro' and of the picaresque novel from its origins in 16th century Spain, via its development and response to Reformation and Counter-Reformation Europe, to the work of Lesage and Defoe.

Alexander A.Parker has held chairs of Spanish Literature in the Universities of Edinburgh, London, Pittsburgh, and Texas.

D1218245

Literature and the Delinquent

The Norman Maccoll Lectures delivered
at the University of Cambridge
in the Easter Term
1965

Literature
and the Delinquent

....

THE PICARESQUE NOVEL IN
SPAIN AND EUROPE
1599-1753

*

ALEXANDER A. PARKER

Edinburgh
AT THE UNIVERSITY PRESS

©
A. A. Parker 1967
EDINBURGH UNIVERSITY PRESS
22 George Square, Edinburgh

First published 1967
Reprinted 1969
Paperback edition 1977
ISBN 0 85224 334 0

Printed in Great Britain by
The Scolar Press Ltd
Ilkley, Yorks

Preface

The University of Cambridge honoured me with the invitation to deliver the Norman Maccoll lectures in April and May 1965. This book incorporates the lectures into a fuller treatment of the subject, but one that is still determined by the form of the lectures, particularly in that it does not try to be anything like a complete survey of its large field. It is an attempt to look at its main aspect from a new angle, with the primary aim of calling the attention of historians and students of English and French literatures to the value of certain Spanish and German novels in the period before Defoe and Lesage. Four lectures were delivered, but it has been more convenient to divide the subject into five chapters. Each lecture has been expanded by amplification rather than by the addition of much new material. The chronological range has, however, been extended from 1735 to 1753 in order to include Fielding and Smollett, for whom no room could be found in the lectures themselves. Despite this expansion there remain very large gaps which I would ask the reader to be indulgent enough to overlook if, as I hope, the total picture is coherent.

I use the word 'picaresque' in its Spanish sense. If its original meaning were restored in the wider context of the European novel as a whole, the term could again become useful in comparative literature, which it has ceased to be. It is a misnomer when used to define structure and not subject-matter. If it is necessary to have a term to distinguish the 'episodic' type of novel, another should be found. The objection that I am writing not about 'novels' at all, but only about 'tales', or 'moral fables', or 'romances', I would dismiss as a niggling terminological point that in no way invalidates either my arguments or my judgements.

I conclude my survey with Smollett because it is still possible, in 1753, to distinguish in his work a clear novelistic tradition constituting a definable section of literary history, although this has already become attenuated. After Smollett one can find, right down to our own day, elements in a multitude of novels, and even whole novels, that can be called 'picaresque', but these are not part of the continuous tradition that starts with *Guzmán de Alfarache*. It may or may not be useful to call such novels as *Huckleberry Finn*, *Felix Krull*, or *Augie March* 'picaresque', but they do not form part of the rise or fall of the historically definable *genre* that is my theme.

In order not to discourage the general reader, who I hope may find interest in this subject, I quote from foreign novels in translation, reproducing the original passages in the Notes. For the same reason I have modernized the spelling of the titles of books as well as of all quotations.

Through the good offices of my colleague, Dr Zděnek Hampejs of the University of Prague, I have received from the author, Dr Oldřich Bělič, a recent book on the Spanish picaresque novel which would not otherwise have come my way: *Španělský Pikareskní Román a Realismus* (Acta Universitatis Carolinae, Prague 1963). This is a substantial monograph, which I am unfortunately unable to read. There is a short summary in Spanish at the end which explains that the book examines the 'realism' of Spanish picaresque novels along the lines followed by Marxist literary criticism in its investigation of the origin of literary realism. The Spanish novels are seen to provide supporting evidence for placing this in the period of the Renaissance; they are interpreted as a literature of social criticism, the *pícaro* being a product of social conditions and his delinquency itself a form of this criticism. The novels are not considered to be 'didactic-religious'; where this aspect is apparent, the contention is that it has been introduced only in order to mislead the censors. This interpretation, by and large, is close to the traditional one, and thus differs from my own. In thanking Dr Hampejs and Dr Bělič for their kindness, I take this opportunity of making known the existence of this work in the hope that some other Hispanist may be able to examine the new evidence and arguments that support this thesis.

I owe a special debt of gratitude to Professor Marcel Bataillon, who has very kindly presented me with offprints of all his recent papers on the Spanish picaresque novel and supplied me with photocopies of the summaries of his lecture courses published in *l'Annuaire du Collège de France*. Professor Bataillon delivered two Special Lectures on this subject to the University of London in 1962, at which I had the privilege of presiding. He there outlined a new approach to the Spanish picaresque *genre* to which I refer in the relevant places of my first two chapters. Since his interpretation still awaits final elaboration I have avoided trespassing on his special field. Our two approaches differ but are, I believe, complementary.

I am grateful also to Dr J.S. Cummins and Dr Peter Murray for help in my search for illustrations, and to Professor W.L. Fichter for sending me a photocopy of a paper from a periodical available in the library of Brown University, but not in that of any British university or in the British Museum.

My colleagues, Professors E.C. Mason and A.J. Steele, have read sections of the book and have generously given me the benefit of their advice, for which I thank them. My thanks are also due to Professor E.M. Wilson, of Cambridge University, whose valuable suggestions I have followed in expanding the original lectures; through him I would also thank the Committee of the Maccoll lectures for their invitation to deliver them. None of these three friends is to be associated with any of the views expressed in these pages.

Last but not least, I must thank Miss Leanne LeCompte for the patience and good humour with which she has typed my manuscript in circumstances often made trying by the relentless pressure of other business.

In Chapter Three I reproduce, as stated in a footnote, the greater part of a paper of mine published in vol. XLII of the *Modern Language Review*. It is reprinted here by permission of the Modern Humanities Research Association and of the Editors, to whom acknowledgements are due.

A. A. P.
Department of Hispanic Studies,
University of Edinburgh
March 1966

Note to Paperback Edition

So much has been published on the picaresque novel since 1966 that some of this book is now out of date. Modifications and additions would be required in the general discussion of the genre, and I would now express some of my judgements differently. I would not retain the sometimes polemical tone : there are clear indications that the term 'picaresque' may now revert in English usage to the sense Hispanists have always given it, and that the significance of the Spanish works is not likely to be minimized any longer, nor their status as 'novels' denied.

University of Texas at Austin
March 1977

Contents

List of Illustrations

for Frances, Emily, and Ian
a souvenir of a reunion
at Berkeley, 12 December 1965
which this book helped to make possible

The illustration facing is the frontispiece to the first edition (1605) of *La pícara Justina*. It represents 'The Ship of the Picaresque Life' sailing on the 'River of Forgetfulness' and steered by Time (whose oar has 'I carry them without their noticing') towards the Port of Death, who holds in his hand the mirror of Disillusion. Bacchus sits on the mast-head, Ceres, Venus and Cupid are portrayed on the sails, and on the pennant is written 'Pleasure impels me'. Idleness lies asleep within the boat; on the prow sits Guzmán de Alfarache as a beggar, with 'poor and happy' written on his satchel; in the centre stands Justina with 'Mother' Celestina in front of her, who is wearing what looks suspiciously like a Cardinal's hat and spectacles (of the kind worn by Quevedo); she holds a large wine-bottle on which is written the proverbial saying *andad hijos*, ironically addressed to lazy people. Justina is dressed in classical garb and is crowned like a Muse; she holds a book on which is inscribed the first line of a song, perhaps traditional, that is found in a play by Lope de Vega:

> *¡Hola!, que me lleva la ola;*
> *¡hola!, que me lleva la mar.*
> *¡Hola!, que llevarme dejo*
> *sin orden y sin consejo,*
> *y que del cielo me alejo,*
> *donde no puedo llegar.*
> *¡Hola!, que me lleva la ola;*
> *¡hola!, que me lleva la mar.*

('Heigh-ho! for the wave is carrying me away. Heigh-ho! for I'm carried away by the sea. Heigh-ho! for I allow myself to be carried, undisciplined and ill-advised; for I'm moving away from heaven, where I can never arrive. Heigh-ho! for the wave is carrying me away. Heigh-ho! for I'm carried away by the sea'.) The ship is being towed by a boat in which Lazarillo is rowing; *siguoles* on his oar is a slip of the engraver's tool for *sigoles* ('I accompany them') or *sigueles* ('he accompanies them'). The 'bull of Salamanca' and the word *oliste* ('you smelt') recall well-known incidents from his story. The letters that accompany the objects surrounding the picture form the phrase *el axuar de la vida picaresca* ('the equipment of the picaresque life'). See pp. 144 and 149.

I

The Genesis of the Picaresque

ALTHOUGH the historical importance of the picaresque tradition in the formation of the modern European novel needs no stressing, the way the subject is commonly presented on the comparative level is now out of focus. Sixty-six years ago Chandler began the publication of his *Romances of Roguery* with the first volume on the picaresque novel in Spain; the intended later volume on the picaresque novel in the rest of Europe was never published. This was a pity, for the two-volume *Literature of Roguery* that followed it was confined to England; out of nearly six hundred pages a mere nine were devoted to Spain by way of introduction.[1] That this came to be thought the right proportion may have been the result of this dissociation of the later study from the earlier, for nowadays historians and critics of the English and French novels tend to give little importance to the Spanish picaresque novels, even to the extent of sometimes minimizing Spain's contribution to the formation of the modern novel by limiting it to the influence of *Don Quixote*. German scholars have not succumbed to the temptation to ignore Spanish literature and so Grimmelshausen is firmly linked to Spain; but the German branch of the picaresque has no impact on the subsequent European novel. Hispanists, for their part, when writing of the Spanish picaresque novel, give only a perfunctory nod towards its European descendants.[2] If I am more venturesome it is because I think there may be some value in the Hispanist's approach to Defoe, Lesage, and Smollett, by which I mean not looking ahead to the later novel that these writers helped to create but looking backwards in order to see what they made of the material they inherited. This focus produces a picture that is different from the traditional and conventional one, and I hope better proportioned. The field is large, but by selecting only the few significant works I hope to be able validly to make my point, which is to suggest that an important section in the history of the European novel needs to undergo revision.

The most recent book on the subject, Robert Alter's *Rogue's Progress: Studies in the Picaresque Novel*,[3] shows what a crying need this really is. Alter claims that the high-water mark of the picaresque genre is reached with *Gil Blas*, *Moll Flanders*, *Roderick Random*, and *Tom Jones*. The study of these novels is prefaced by a mere ten pages on the Spanish origins of the genre, which are *Lazarillo de Tormes* and nothing else. This is not a picaresque novel at all in the full sense of the term; in any case, between it and the First Part of *Gil Blas* there is a gap of 161 years. Since his book is not a historical survey, Alter was not obliged to bridge this gap, but if it is bridged, his four chosen novels can appear in rather a different light.

Whether as cause or effect, the present minimization of the importance of the Spanish picaresque novel in the history of literature is accompanied by a remarkable vagueness concerning the nature of such a novel. For instance, the section on the picaresque in the *Reader's Guide to Prose Fiction*[4] lists fifteen novels as examples of the genre. Only two, *Gil Blas* and *Roderick Random*, come into the category as it used to be understood; the rest range from *All Men are Brothers* (a Chinese novel of the thirteenth century), through *Don Quixote* and *Candide*, to *The Good Companions*. Since nowadays the word 'picaresque' is in fact commonly stretched 'to mean any novel in which the hero takes a journey whose course plunges him into all sorts, conditions and classes of men',[5] we need not wonder at *Don Quixote*'s being classified as a picaresque novel or even at the term being applied to *The Pilgrim's Progress*, though we may still wonder what purpose is supposedly served by lumping so many disparate works together. But even more surprising than what we nowadays find included in the category is what we find excluded. A critic setting out to prove the influence of Quevedo's *Vida del buscón* on Smollett's *Count Fathom* laments the fact that the *Buscón* 'is still commonly mistaken for a picaresque novel', which it cannot be because it is a 'moral tale'.[6] Since in Spanish literature *La vida del buscón* is the peak of the picaresque tradition, it is clear that our terminology has become ridiculously confused. It must be straightened out, and the only way to do this is to go back to what the picaresque novel was, and what this Spanish word meant, at the beginning.

¶ 'Picaroon' and 'picaresque' have been traditionally defined as 'rogue' and 'roguish', and the picaresque novels have generally been called romances of roguery. These are unfortunate terms, because 'rogue' nowadays tends to imply mischievousness or waggishness. Hence we find such definitions of the picaresque novel as this: 'a type of satirical fiction originating in Spain in the sixteenth century and having an amusing rogue or vagabond as hero'.[7] That the word is losing or has already lost its original connotation is also demonstrated by the fact that Robert Alter takes it as axiomatic that 'the picaroon may have natural inclinations towards roguery, but he is not by nature a scoundrel...he demonstrates some strength in the virtues of the heart.... For perhaps the most basic assumption underlying the picaresque world view is the conviction that while life is hard, life is also good....Without this supposition that man is basically decent, or at least that some men are decent, the picaresque virtues of compassion and companionship would be totally inexplicable.'[8] Anyone familiar with Spanish literature can only gasp at the phrase 'the picaresque virtues of compassion and companionship'. Alter can write it without turning a hair, because by jumping the 161 years between *Lazarillo de Tormes* and *Gil Blas* he excludes from his account of the picaroon all the Spanish examples, since Lázaro (to whom the phrase can to some extent apply) is not a *pícaro* at all.[9] The first protagonist of a novel to whom the word is applied in the novel itself is Guzmán de Alfarache, who is a very different type of character.

Philologists are still not agreed on the etymology of *pícaro*. The word is first documented in 1525 with the sense of 'kitchen boy', but twenty years later it already meant 'evil living'. The first Dictionary of the Spanish Academy in 1726, which reflects the usage of the seventeenth century, defines *pícaro* as 'low, vicious, deceitful, dishonourable and shameless'.[10] 'Rogue' seems to me now quite inadequate as an equivalent for this; I prefer the term 'delinquent' as being the word that in current usage best expresses the *pícaro* of Spanish seventeenth-century literature. By this I mean an offender against the moral and civil laws; not a vicious criminal such as a gangster or a murderer, but someone who is dishonourable and anti-social in a much less violent way. The fact that the word delinquent is now so frequently associated with juveniles makes it particularly appropriate as a rendering for the *pícaro* of the novels. The word and what it denotes is nowadays very much in the forefront of our social conscience, and this also makes its use appropriate for my purpose. The revaluation of the Spanish picaresque novels will be helped by the realization that their subject-matter has an actuality that the traditional interpretation of the genre obscures. Our contemporary society and much of our post-war literature are preoccupied with delinquency. We are aware of teenagers whom a sociologist has recently called 'the unattached', and whose characteristics are worth noting here because many will recur, *mutatis mutandis*, in the pages that follow:

their inability to join a youth organization was no more than one expression of a much wider pattern of unstable behaviour....Much of the unstable pattern seems to be due to frustrations of various origins, which could usually be traced back to a single or a combination of factors. These were emotionally poor home background....In some cases failure to achieve unrealistic or unattainable goals they had set for themselves or had had set for them caused frustration or boredom.... Another characteristic in all areas was a general inability to postpone immediate pleasure for the sake of future gain. It came out in attitudes towards money (saving and spending) and in an inability to undertake training for vocational advancement. With some young people, on the surface at least, 'bumming' had become a recognized, accepted, and valued way of life...a hand-to-mouth philosophy governed the lives of these youths; leisure-time interests were short-spanned, constantly changing, and interspersed liberally with periods of boredom and apathy; friendships suffered because they were incapable of sustaining any effective feelings of obligation or consideration for others...excitement was often sought through delinquency: avoiding payment of rail fares, petty thieving, entering cinemas and dance halls without payment, violation of property....[11]

In our contemporary literature we are also familiar with characters who are, at their worst, psychotic deviationists, at their least harmful what Miss M. C. Bradbrook has called 'the Non-U on [their] way up'.[12] In the forms of an unattached outsider or an unscrupulous gate-crasher, the delinquent is the centre of the literature I am going to discuss, for it is in the Spanish picaresque tradition that he first makes his entry into the European novel as a collective image. His importance in the history of the novel is well known, though not always openly acknowledged. The modern novel is born when realism first supplants the fanciful idealistic romance, namely the novels of chivalry, and later the pastoral novels and the pseudo-historical romances. This realism is ushered in with the Spanish *pícaro*, who relates his life-story, generally from his childhood, in the form of an autobiography constituting an episodic narrative rather than a unified one. The autobiographical form, although adopted by the majority of the picaresque novelists, is not essential; the distinguishing feature of the *genre* is the atmosphere of delinquency. This begins in a setting of low life but generally ascends the social scale; the origins of the protagonist are usually disreputable; he is either born or plunged as a youth into an environment of cheating and thieving, and learns to make his way in the world by cheating and thieving in his turn.

¶ The history of the *genre* is briefly as follows. The first novel that had a direct, though belated, influence in creating it was the anonymous *Lazarillo de Tormes* of 1554. Although this is generally considered the prototype of the picaresque novel, it is better called the precursor[13]; the prototype is the very much longer *Guzmán de Alfarache* by Mateo Alemán (1547–1614?), whose First Part was published in 1599 and the Second Part in 1604. This established the characteristics of form and content which *Lazarillo* had adumbrated. With *Guzmán de Alfarache* realism became the norm for the Spanish novel. It was followed immediately by *Don Quixote*, Part I in 1605 and Part II in 1615; but this masterpiece, although it enormously widened the scope of the new realism, neither equalled *Guzmán de Alfarache* in popularity nor shaped the novel that was to come. Thanks to the earlier work, the picaresque became the main novelistic tradition. From 1605 onwards, quite a large number of these novels were published and the idealistic novel was supplanted. *Don Quixote* is itself the last Spanish novel of chivalry, and no pastoral novel by an author of any repute was published after 1608. But the picaresque novel itself had only a relatively short life in Spain; the last one that can be properly so called was *Estebanillo González* of 1646. After that date the *genre* had its vogue abroad.

Guzmán de Alfarache was very quickly translated into French, German and English. In Germany, in a curiously indirect way, it produced its greatest descendant, Grimmelshausen's *Simplicissimus* (1669). In France and England the *genre* had a longer history. Several of the Spanish novels, in addition to *Guzmán*, were adapted into French and translated into English, and were instrumental in giving birth to French and English realism. In France this occurred at the very height of the vogue of the heroic romance; but although both the *Francion* of Sorel (1622 and 1641) and the *Roman comique* (1651) of Scarron owe much to the Spanish picaresque tradition, they are not themselves novels of delinquency and are much closer to Cervantes than to Alemán and his followers. The picaresque *genre* is represented in France above all by Lesage, whose translations and adaptations of Spanish works were followed by his own *Gil Blas*, the three parts of which were published in 1715, 1724, and 1735.

In England, although Nashe's *Unfortunate Traveller* (1594) gave early promise of an independent realism, the French heroic romances held sway for the greater part of the seventeenth century. Mabbe's translation of *Guzmán de Alfarache*, under the title of *The Rogue* (1622), was followed by *The English Rogue* of Head and Kirkman, in three parts (1665, 1668, and 1671). Biographies, real or fictitious, of members of the criminal class became popular, and Defoe then emerged. *Colonel Jack* and *Moll Flanders* both appeared in 1722; the latter is generally considered the best of Defoe's novels of delinquency and marks the peak of the picaresque tradition in England, almost exactly contemporaneous with *Gil Blas* in France. Smollett is still within the tradition with *Roderick Random* (1748) and *Ferdinand Count Fathom* (1753).

Lesage and Defoe have comparable positions in their respective literatures. Lesage is hailed by French critics as the creator of the novel of manners; according to British critics, Defoe marks the turning-point in the history of fiction, and he is acclaimed as the founder of the modern novel. Both are said to bring to fruition the movements in existence before their time; the implication, therefore, is that these were all primitive or imperfect. The Spanish picaresque tradition, from which they both derive, is conceded only a limited value, that of merely helping to pave the way for the masters of realism, who, after Defoe, are Fielding and Smollett. Thus, the standard judgement of histories of literature on *Gil Blas* in relation to its tradition is that the Spanish picaresque novels remain only Spanish, while with *Gil Blas* the genre is universalized. Even *Don Quixote*, when placed in this comparative historical context, is sometimes disparaged by, for example, being excluded from the definition of the novel because of its episodic structure or its satirical intentions.[14]

The general picture of the development of the modern novel is drawn along the following lines: the idealistic romances bred 'anti-romances' in Spain, which by a natural reaction presented the crude and sordid. These anti-romances were either implicitly satirical of all heroism, like the picaresque novels, or deliberate parodies, like *Don Quixote*; in either case they emphasized the comic in order to counter the solemnity they satirized. Realism, emerging as anti-romance in Spain, then became established in its own right in France and England as an objective means of depicting human life and studying manners, free from satirical and comic preoccupations.

One might not quarrel with the view that puts Lesage and Defoe at the peak of development and Spanish picaresque novels below them if literary values and significance do, indeed, reside mainly in form and technique, where literary historians have so often tended to look for them—in this case, in the creation of unified plots, in lifelike characterization, and in the exercise of detached and accurate observation. By such criteria the Spanish picaresque novel would offer little more than antecedents of the great European novel, which would thus begin in the eighteenth century. But novels, to be significant, should offer something more than mere technique and accuracy of realistic description; they should tell us something important about human nature and human life. If, with this criterion, we examine the history of the picaresque novel in Europe from Alemán to Defoe and Lesage, it is possible that we may not find a steady ascent; a different order of values may, in fact, be discernible.

Before the possible lines of such an examination can be sketched, it is necessary to point to four misleading assumptions that have helped to prevent the best of the Spanish picaresque novels from receiving, in the sphere of comparative literature, the serious consideration they deserve. The first is the belief that the picaresque genre arose in Spain because Spain at that time was the country in which social conditions were most conducive to the production of delinquents in large numbers. The second is the assumption that the picaresque novels are essentially comic, since their authors turned to the real-life phenomenon of the delinquent in order to produce a satirical counterblast to the romances. The third is the belief that, since the novels were born out of prevailing social conditions, the society they portray is more important than the individual characters they present as protagonists. The last misconception is that, since the novels are essentially humorous and deal with unsavoury material, they have no real moral interest, any avowed moral intentions being hypocritical, or at best conventional, lip-service to social propriety. The first of these assumptions is practically universal; the other three derive from Chandler. Since his three volumes are still the only extensive study of the picaresque novel on a comparative basis, his critical opinions on the Spanish novels have continued to be influential, especially among English-speaking historians and critics, even though we have for the most part long since abandoned the critical approach to literature which he exemplified sixty-six years ago. An examination of some of the novels will in due course present evidence to refute the last two of these assumptions, but a discussion of the first two is appropriate in this chapter by way of introduction to the *genre* and its genesis.

¶For nearly a hundred years it has been constantly affirmed that the picaresque novel mirrors a country in decline, poverty-stricken, morally corrupt, and therefore the breeding-ground of beggars and delinquents.[15] Contemporary records can certainly give a depressing picture of social and economic conditions in the Spain of the sixteenth and seventeenth centuries. It is immaterial to wonder how distorted such pictures might be by one-sided selection of evidence, since it is just as easy to produce similar pictures of other countries. Evidence of this kind is of little value unless it is comparative; and how can we assess with any confidence that conditions in Spain were so much worse than those in other countries that it was appropriate for novels of delinquency to be born there and not elsewhere? None of the numerous authorities who see this as the axiomatic origin of the picaresque ever refer their readers to Ribton-Turner's *History of Vagrants and Vagrancy*,[16] which gives the complete European picture.

Cervantes, in his Exemplary Novel *Rinconete y Cortadillo*, published in 1613 but mentioned in 1605 in the First Part of *Don Quixote*, portrays the thieves of Seville as organized and disciplined along the lines of a medieval guild; and there is evidence to prove that this picture is not exaggerated. But there was nothing peculiar to Spain in this: for a long time criminals and vagabonds had formed guilds all over Europe, with masters and apprentices, rules and registers, the Masters assigning tasks to the individual members and dividing the booty. The most complex development of these guilds is found in France. Ribton-Turner thus describes it:

In these two reigns [Francis I and Henry II] flourished in all their cynical insolence the associations of beggars known under the name of *bélistres* (rascals). At the top of the tree was the king of the *Bélistres*, who bore the title of *Coesre* or Arch-rogue. Then came the *cagous* (master thieves entrusted with the education of novices) and *archisuppôts* (retired leading thieves), governors or intendants of the provinces of the kingdom of rascality; they counterfeited persons of rank ruined or robbed, and crippled soldiers. They were sometimes called the gentry of the *short sword*, on account of the scissors which they used for cutting purses. Numerous inferior ranks completed this organization, which at the time of its dispersal in 1656 comprised 40,000 beggars in Paris alone, living in eleven *Cours des Miracles*, which Victor Hugo later made familiar, so called from the miraculous way in which the blind, deformed, and lame who lived there recovered from their ailments as soon as they reached home.[17]

In Germany, the *Liber vagatorum* (*c.* 1520)[18] divided beggars into twenty-eight classes according to the different ways of cheating and robbing. In addition to common ones like the blind beggars, the cripples, or the sham begging priests, there was the class of the learned beggars, young scholars, or students on the tramp, and the class of the pretended noblemen who claimed to have lost all their possessions through war, fire, or captivity. In Italy, a century later, there were thirty-four classes of delinquent beggars, according to *Il vagabondo* of Giacinto Nobili (1627).[19] Most of these exploited religious devotions or superstitions, but there were refined classes like the *poveri vergognosi*, respectable poor who pretended to be too ashamed to beg; there was also the ingenious class of the *testatori*, who pretended to be ill and to bequeath money to those who protected them. No Spanish picaresque novel reveals anything like the range and ingenuity of confidence tricks listed for Germany and Italy by these two books.

The rogue literature of Elizabethan and Jacobean England is extensive. There are classifications and full descriptions of the types of cheating beggars in, for instance, *The Fraternity of Vagabonds* (1561) by John Awdeley, and *A Caveat for Common Cursitors* (1566) by Thomas Harman. Dekker's *The*

Bellman of London and *Lantern and Candlelight*, both of 1608, are fascinating accounts of London's underworld. On the social conditions they mirror, their modern editor states:

Whatever exaggeration we may discover in panicky appeals for rigorous deeds, or read into official acts and regulations, it is clear that a problem of the first magnitude did exist, not only in the minds of justices and legislators, but also in actual fact. All accounts affirm that the number of beggars was prodigious; thieves abounded everywhere; and in the unruly north their bands were still a menace to the villages after the borderland ceased to be a frontier.[20]

The state of public morals in Spain at the beginning of her decline could not have been worse than in England at the threshold of her greatness, if indeed as bad; it has been said that under Elizabeth the state of public and private life revealed 'a consistency of moral decay which can hardly be paralleled in English history – the general gloom is only lit up here and there by individual characters.... The bishops were avaricious, the parochial clergy fell far short of their calling, and the administration of local government was deplorably corrupt. Purity, honesty, fair dealing and justice do not flourish under such conditions.'[21]

To help remedy this state of affairs the Queen's government had in 1597 (39 Eliz. c. 4) prescribed banishment abroad for incorrigible and dangerous rogues, without specifying the destinations; six years later an Order in Council defined the places of transportation as not only across the Atlantic but also 'France, Germany, Spain and the Low Countries'.[22] I have not found evidence that this was ever actually carried out as regards the European continent, but, in view of the traditional explanation of the Spanish picaresque novel, the thought of England in 1603 exporting surplus rogues to Spain is delightful.

It is surely unquestionable that, if the new realistic novel of the sixteenth century needed a society in which vagrancy and delinquency were prominent, it could just as easily have been born in any other country as in Spain. The material was abundantly to hand everywhere. In England it was, in fact, utilized by the writers represented in *The Elizabethan Underworld* for character sketches and genre-paintings full of a racy realism; yet these are tracts not novels. The social incentive to observe and record was there, but the particular incentive needed to transform this into novels was lacking. That Spain felt the incentive must mean that conditions or influences prevailed or operated there which were peculiar to Spain and therefore cultural rather than economic.

Two possible non-economic conditions have been suggested to account for the picaresque novel. The first is that maid-of-all-work in much speculation by Spaniards on their own culture – the national character. This, it has often been held, is compounded of the chivalrous, the mystical, and the picaresque. The last of these qualities, which is the obverse of the other two, is promoted to the status of a typically Spanish attitude to life, namely the tendency to shirk or evade responsibility.[23] This really means no more than that Spaniards are human; but in any case, even if this is a trait universally characteristic of the Spanish people, it still remains necessary to ask why it produced a distinctive novelistic convention only during a particular half-century of that people's history, and not before or after. The second explanation has been put forward by Américo Castro as part of his general interpretation of Spanish civilization. Thirty years ago he had suggested that the picaresque novel arose as the expression of the social resentment of the underdog against the privileged classes[24]; now he tends to equate this with the resentment of the convert Jews against a society which, because it viewed them with mistrust, closed against them all the doors of social advancement. The justification for this is that Mateo Alemán was of Jewish descent; Castro now takes it for granted that the author of *Lazarillo de Tormes* must also have been a Jew,[25] although there is no evidence for this whatever. Such speculations are not only rash, they really get us nowhere; there is nothing in *Guzmán de Alfarache* which requires to be explained by its author's being a Jew: its pessimism and disenchantment with life are the mark of the new age which it is ushering in.[26]

It would be pointless to deny that there were economic and religious strains in the social life of Spain and that these could be reflected in literature, but it is not easy to assess the influence of such things on the rise of a new literary *genre*. There must, of course, have been some connexion between its emergence and the social life of the country at that particular period, but it is much safer to look for signs of the connexion in the literature itself than to fall back on national psychology, or to postulate an economic explanation or the resentment of an oppressed Jewish minority. The problem is essentially one of literary history.

Marcel Bataillon gives a much surer direction to Castro's theory when he states that what should be investigated is not the racial ancestry of the novelists, which it is usually impossible to uncover, but the part played in the novels themselves by the consciousness of 'purity of blood'. The various social tensions to which this gave rise, especially in connexion with social advancement on the part of men of bourgeois origin, he sees reflected ironically and satirically in the narratives of the novels and in the fictional ancestries of the picaroons. This will be the central aspect in the interpretation of the Spanish picaresque novel that he is evolving; it will suggest that the contact between the novels and contemporary society is on a different social plane from the one where it has traditionally been placed.[27] There is, however, another significant way in which the picaresque novels reveal a direct connexion with contemporary social life; and this, while we await Bataillon's promised study, can cast light on the question of the origin of the *genre*.

¶In his Exemplary Novel *La ilustre fregona* (*The Illustrious Kitchenmaid*), published in 1613, Cervantes writes of two youths of good families who, travelling from their homes to the University of Salamanca in the company of their tutor, give him the slip in order to escape to Seville to lead the lives of picaroons. One of them had done this before.

> Carriazo might have been thirteen or a little more at the time when, solely from a vagabond inclination, without receiving from his parents any ill-treatment to force him to the step, but simply for his own pleasure and fancy, he played truant, as children say, from his father's house, and went forth through the world, so satisfied with an untrammelled life, that, in the midst of the hardships and miseries it brings with it, he did not miss the abundance of his home, nor did trudging on foot weary him, nor cold injure him, nor heat tire him. For him all seasons of the year were a sweet and temperate spring; he slept as well among the thrashed corn as on cushions; he buried himself with as much pleasure in a loft of an inn as if he were lying between two holland sheets. In short, he fared so well with the occupation of a *pícaro* that he could have lectured from a chair in the faculty to the famous Alfarache.[28]

Returning home after three years of this life, he feels such nostalgia for his former care-free and adventurous existence that he persuades a friend to play truant from the university. The greatest attraction for such boys and youths was the tunny fishery of Andalusia. 'Here', says Cervantes, 'come or send many fathers of quality to seek their sons, and they find them, and the latter feel as much their removal from this life as if their fathers were carrying them off to put them to death.'[29]

That Cervantes was here reporting a social fact is all the more likely since his two boys may actually have existed. Their names occur in the matriculation registers of Salamanca for 1581-4. Cervantes gives their residence as Burgos; the surname of the original truant was, in fact, the name of a leading family of that city, and the name Cervantes gives to the boy's father was the name of a magistrate of Burgos in 1569 and

1570.[30] Cervantes may therefore have recalled an actual event; in any case, it seems certain that the attraction of freedom, of an unrestrained and anarchical existence, could in real life outweigh the comforts of a settled domestic existence.

A number of contemporary writers, in the context of the picaresque, sing the praises of the free life, and some of the picaroons themselves do so also. Writing of the time when, as a boy, he had arrived in Madrid and found that his life was his own, Guzmán de Alfarache calls it 'glorious freedom' to be able to eat one's bread without having to receive it from another's hand, since the bread that is given to one is always 'bread of sorrow, bread of suffering' even when it is one's own father who gives it.[31]

There is a dramatic interlude entitled *Testamento del pícaro pobre* (*The Poor Picaroon's Last Will*), which was published in 1614 but probably written before 1605. It is a conventional farce with humour of a simple kind: a picaroon, having been promised wine, is given water to drink; he dies of the shock, having just time to confess his sins and make his will. The interlude finishes with a sonnet in praise of the picaroon's life, which begins: 'To enjoy freedom and to live content; to dream one is a king while dressed in rags; to eat pheasants though they be but garlic, and to have only thoughts that are gay', and so on.[32] A poem of the same period entitled *La vida del pícaro* (*The Picaroon's Life*), after many stanzas in similar vein, concludes: 'My pen was running away, yet I still fall short in praising the life I yearn for.... Only the picaroon dies a successful man, because, desiring nothing from the time he was born, he has all his capital saved up.... His lofty castles are the bare ground, stable as long as the world endures, storing all the treasures of Heaven.'[33]

In view of evidence of this kind, the picaresque novel has been interpreted by Frutos Gómez as the promulgation of a 'philosophy of freedom'.[34] Like its elder sister, the pastoral novel, it inherits from the Renaissance the ideal of the return to nature, an autonomous life, simple, happy, free from care and unhampered by the conventions of a complex social order. But while the shepherds of literature cut themselves off from society in an Arcadia where this freedom and simplicity can be imaginatively achieved, the picaroon has to cut himself off from society while living within it: he is thus an 'outsider' in our modern sense. The difference between the pastoral and the picaresque is, according to Frutos Gómez, that the former derives from Italian humanism while the latter derives from Erasmus's *Praise of Folly* (1509) through the reforming movements that made for a simplified religion of the spirit unencumbered by complicated observances, preaching poverty and contempt for the world and its honours. The picaroon inherited this ideal, but persecuted by society as an outcast he represented the degeneration of the ideal into an embittered and resentful cynicism within the moral vacuum of what had now, with the picaresque novels, come to be a purely negative literature.

This is not the place to discuss this thesis, which has more to support it than this summary can indicate. Spanish literature in the sixteenth and seventeenth centuries abounds in praise of the simple life, a theme whose many facets still await a proper study. This longing for a free and natural existence is deeply rooted in human nature, and it can clearly take negative or socially antagonistic forms as well as positive ones. Undoubtedly, behind the picaroons' praise of their free life we can sometimes detect a note of nostalgia on the part of their creators. The clearest example of this is one of which Frutos Gómez was unaware, an intended Third Part to *Guzmán de Alfarache*, written about 1650 but not published till this century. Its author was a Portuguese nobleman, the Marquis of Montebelo. The dedication, which is to the errand boys of Madrid, opens with the conventional praise of their care-free existence but soon turns into what is clearly the resentment of a nobleman against the difficulties of keeping up his position. 'You can dress as you please', writes the Marquis,

> you eat out of your own hand and no one kisses it to

deceive you.... You have no claims to support; no
lawsuits keep you awake at night.... You may stain
your clothes, but you cannot stain your honour. You
are not bound by the laws of politeness.... In short,
you are the rulers of your own wills, the administrators
of your own income... a state exempt from taxation, a
nation without wars.... May God preserve you from
ever becoming gentlemen.[35]

Clearly, then, the pleasure that law-abiding readers found in
the delinquents of literature was not only the excitement of
vicariously discarding a moral restraint; it could also be the
vicarious easing of a social restraint.

But what of the delinquents themselves in the eyes of their
creators? The social problem that is the starting-point for *La
ilustre fregona* of Cervantes (the boys who run away from
home); the satisfaction that Guzmán felt when he was at last
his own master: these clearly represent natural adolescent reactions against excessive discipline or a boring domestic existence. Even today Spanish home life in the middle classes
can, by our standards, be excessively conservative and rigid;
around 1600 it must have been very strict and very puritanical
–no wonder if some teenage boys preferred the freedom of the
tunny fishery to the restraints of respectable home life in small
provincial cities.

None-the-less, to explain the picaresque novel as arising
solely from nostalgia for social freedom seems to me ultimately
misguided because it disregards the context in which the theme
of freedom invariably occurs in the literature of the period;
the context is not that of approval but of condemnation. All
the praises of freedom referred to above, with the exception of
the Marquis of Montebelo, are ironical. The Spaniards of
1600 knew very clearly how attractive an anarchical freedom
can appear to be to the young; but they also knew, even more
clearly, the difference between the responsible freedom that
chooses discipline and the licence that rejects it. For every
instance in which the theme of freedom appears in the Spanish

literature of the sixteenth and seventeenth centuries as praise of the natural life, there are ninety-nine in which it appears as a question of moral discipline. This is expressed most explicitly in the religious literature, which in lyrical poems and morality plays presents from first to last countless allegories in which man enters into the world along what he thinks is the path of freedom, only to find that it is the road of enslavement to passion and the senses. This is exactly how Alemán presents the problem of delinquency in *Guzmán de Alfarache*, and this is the cultural and literary context into which the rise of this type of realistic fiction should be put.

¶The picaresque novel thus arises as an exposition of the theme of freedom, including the concept of moral freedom. It does not arise as anti-romance in the sense of an implicit parody of idealistic fiction; and this is the second assumption I want to question: that the picaresque novel is essentially comic. I see it as no more than a half-truth or even a quarter-truth as regards Spain, but the comic anti-romance nature of the new realistic novel is, of course, true of France. *Francion* of Sorel and *Roman comique* of Scarron have this character. In Sorel the parody aim becomes explicit in his *le Berger extravagant* (1627), which burlesques the pastoral novel *Astrée* (1607-27). The Spanish precedent for the comic ironical quality of these novels is, however, *Don Quixote*, not the picaresque. The first Spanish novels can indeed be considered, historically, as reactions against pastoral novels and novels of chivalry, but as alternatives not as satires. We find in them no sign of any parody of idealistic fiction, such as constitutes the avowed purpose of *Don Quixote*. Yet it is Cervantes who gives us our clue: he constantly stresses that he is offering a *true* chivalry novel to supplant those that are *untrue*. In attacking this type of literature as untrue, Cervantes was far from being original; he was repeating views that had been first expressed in Spain quite early in the sixteenth century and insistently reiterated up to his time.

Renaissance humanists like Luis Vives or Juan de Valdés attacked the novels of chivalry for their improbabilities and impossibilities, for being untrue to human nature and human experience. The literary ideal of Valdés, in particular, was coherence within a framework of events and characters that could happen and exist in reality; in short, an ideal of realism that was not then, in the 1530s, being exemplified in fiction. These humanists were part of the movement of religious reform inspired by Erasmus who, as Marcel Bataillon has shown, was more influential in Spain than elsewhere.[36] These Spanish Erasmian humanists did produce between 1530 and 1560 a literature, some of it not published till the nineteenth century, that within a more or less realistic social framework satirized the moral and religious hypocrisy of the times.[37] It is out of this climate of a social satire born of the urge to religious reform that *Lazarillo de Tormes* emerged in 1554.[38] This famous little work provided the form for the future picaresque novel –an autobiographical narration with an episodic plot; but it was to be forty-five years before this form was to be used again.

In the meantime, the protests that the Erasmian humanists had made against idealistic literature in the first half of the sixteenth century were repeated, more vigorously and influentially, in the second half of the century by the churchmen who continued the movement of religious reform, now modified and canalized by the Council of Trent into the Counter-Reformation. They levelled their criticism against the new pastoral romances as well as the novels of chivalry. Criticism

---

[1.] Nicholas Jennings, alias Blunt, an Elizabethan begging impostor. He was sentenced to stand 'upon the pillory, both in his ugly and handsome attire; and after that went in the mill while his ugly picture was a drawing; and then was whipped at a cart's tail through London…And his picture remaineth in Bridewell for a monument.' His story is related in *A Caveat or Warning for Common Cursitors* (1566) by Thomas Harman, and his picture was published in *The Groundwork of Cony-catching* (1592). See pp. 10-12.

of the unreality of this literature had now widened into criticism of its irresponsibility, first because it taught its readers no truth about life–ignoring in particular everything connected with religion–and secondly because it encouraged what we now call escapism. The Dominican writer, Luis de Granada, put this clearly enough when he said that the popularity of novels of chivalry was due to the fact that women, identifying themselves with Oriana and other heroines, secretly felt themselves to be deserving of the service and heroic prowess of knights; men readers for their part enjoyed the vicarious excitement of witnessing heroic and dangerous deeds in their imaginations.[39] The Spanish churchmen of the Counter-Reformation, in pursuit of the policy laid down by the Council of Trent of re-imbuing literature with religious and moral values, therefore advocated replacing the untruthful romances by a literature that would be truthful. By this they meant one that would promulgate the truths of the Christian faith and a sense of moral responsibility based upon the actual problems of real life and upon the acceptance, through self-knowledge instead of escapism, of the actual weakness rather than the potential heroism of human nature.

These Spanish churchmen did supply this alternative literature. Some of the religious writings of the last thirty years of the sixteenth century are the influence that, in my opinion, can alone explain the transition from idealism to realism in the novel. To take one example: in 1588 the Augustinian friar Pedro Malón de Chaide published his book on the conversion of St Mary Magdalen[40] as a story of divine love, explicitly offered in the preface as an alternative to the stories of profane love in the pastoral novels like *Diana* (1559). Both the contacts and the contrasts with the pastoral novel are enlightening. *Diana* had been a treatise on Neo-Platonic love following the

[2.] Scenes of picaresque life in the seventeenth century. An illustration to *La vida del buscón* in the Verdussen (Antwerp 1699) edition of *Obras de Don Francisco de Quevedo*.

doctrine of Leone Ebreo: the *Conversión de la Magdalena* is, in its First Part, the finest treatise on the Platonic conception of love ever written in Spanish; but it is a Christianized Platonism that does not stop on the level of man's love for woman, but makes the whole of creation ascend to God in response to love. Secondly, *Diana* had a heroine, or several heroines, exemplifying true love; Malón de Chaide has one also, but a historical woman, the Mary Magdalen of the Gospels, who according to tradition had been a prostitute before being touched by the love of Christ. The repentant prostitute becomes the new heroine of love; in that she was a sinner she represents, as none of the heroines of fiction had done, the reality of human experience; in her answer to the call of a higher love she represents the ideal – an attainable ideal if, as in her case, repentance is made for sin. In Spanish literature there is thus a shift away from the confident reliance on human values to the recognition of the essential weakness of human nature, which must be disciplined and conquered before any ideal can be attained. The heroine of literature is now a sinner.

Eleven years later, in 1599, Mateo Alemán published the First Part of *Guzmán de Alfarache* – the first fully-developed picaresque novel and the first full-length realistic novel in European literature.[41] It satisfied the demands of the Counter-Reformation in that, being realistic, it was truthful and responsible. It served the ends of truth in that the story explicitly illustrated the doctrines of sin, repentance and salvation, the hero being one who, like Mary Magdalen, goes in search of the love of the world only to land in infamy, but who is able in his degradation to respond, like her, to the higher love. The heroes of romance are thus replaced by a picaroon – a thief, criminal, and galley-slave – who yet wins through to regeneration in the end.

Only in this sense did the Spanish picaresque novel arise as a reaction to the romances – not as satire or parody, but as a deliberate alternative, a 'truthful' literature in response to the explicit demands of the Counter-Reformation. In employing narrative realism to fulfil this task Alemán turned to the only precedent available, that of *Lazarillo de Tormes*, but he expands its primitive novelistic structure almost out of all recognition.[42] Part of the expansion lies in combining the narrative with a didactic treatise. The two are not fused but are developed side by side, the treatise being interpolated into the fictional plot as a series of discursive digressions. Alemán did not get this dualistic form from *Lazarillo*; it is the pattern of the religious writings of the age, particularly of the lives of saints. The *Conversión de la Magdalena* has precisely this form, although more loosely knit and more unbalanced, of intermingled digressions and sections of narrative. A final link between it and *Guzmán de Alfarache* is that Alemán's novel has an attack on secular love literature, notably the pastoral novel,[43] and the prologue to Malón's work contains the best known diatribe of this kind. This does not mean that Malón was Alemán's source, but it does mean that the latter's novel was born from the literature and out of the culture that the former exemplifies. The picaresque novel has its origins in the movement of religious reform. An illuminating confirmation of this contention is the statement by Luis de Valdés, in his preface to the Second Part of *Guzmán de Alfarache*, that a learned Augustinian friar had praised the First Part in a public ceremony at the University of Salamanca as being the best book of secular literature that had yet appeared.

Guzmán de Alfarache was a best-seller both in Spain and abroad. Its popularity in its own country surpassed even that of *Don Quixote*. The new *genre* thus came into existence immediately. Three years later an apocryphal Second Part by Juan Martí was published (1602); Alemán's genuine Second Part followed in 1604,[44] *La pícara Justina* by López de Úbeda in 1605, and picaresque novels continued to appear, although at longer intervals, for the next forty years.

Lazarillo de Tormes had no line of succession comparable to this. Apart from an anonymous apocryphal Second Part that appeared in Antwerp in 1555 and which is not worth reading,

it remained isolated for forty-five years. This fact alone makes
it impossible to call it the first example of a new *genre*. It was,
however, part of what might have become a line of satirical-
social novels very different from the new contemporary pastoral had not religious developments cut this short. The new
censorship consequent on the persecution of Protestants, and
the discredit and suspicion that fell on the followers of Erasmus for their closeness to Lutheranism, meant that of these
fictional works only *Lazarillo de Tormes* saw the light, and it
survived subsequently only in an expurgated form. Two
others of the same period survived in MS, but these have no
close affinities with *Lazarillo de Tormes* in either subject-
matter or form; they do not, therefore, suggest a picaresque
genre in the making.[45] *Lazarillo de Tormes* was thus a precursor
of a *genre* that still had a long time to wait before being born.
None-the-less, it fits exactly into the picture here sketched of
the genesis of the picaresque novel, for it, too, was born of the
movement of religious reform. Marcel Bataillon, the great
authority on Spanish Erasmianism, has denied that it is an
Erasmian work because, although it is anticlerical and satirizes
the preaching of indulgences, it does not promulgate the positive doctrine of the religion of the spirit.[46] But it is difficult to
see how it could have done so, since it is autobiographical in
form, and the narrator has cynically to expose himself at the
end as accepting, for the sake of material comfort, a dishonourable marriage; such a man could preach no positive spiritual
doctrine. Manuel Asensio, who has raised this objection, has
added plausible support to the contention that *Lazarillo de
Tormes* was the work of an Erasmian humanist.[47] To me it
seems clear that it has as close a connexion with the movement
of religious reform in the early part of the century as *Guzmán
de Alfarache* has with the movement of religious revival at the
end of the century. The emergence of the picaresque *genre* in
Spain is explained more satisfactorily by this literary-cultural
background than by economic conditions, Jewish *conversos*, or
qualities in the national character.

Erasmian humanism or the Spanish Counter-Reformation did not, of course, produce the realistic technique that makes the picaresque novel more alive and modern than the types of fiction it supplanted. The technique as such was not new: it had been exemplified magnificently by Fernando de Rojas in *La Celestina* at the end of the fifteenth century, to go no further back. What the movement of religious reform gave to the novel was the 'truthfulness' and 'responsibility' that literature was seen to need but which could not be found in idealistic fiction –the desire to portray men as they are, in order to open the eyes of the readers of literature to the shortcomings of human nature, and their minds to the need to prevent or remedy them; what in practice produced a serious interest in delinquency. It is realism in this sense that the novel acquires from this source. Realism in the sense of technique was required by literary conventions and theory, which did not permit a delinquent to be presented in any other way. He could only belong to the plane of everyday reality from which nobility, heroism, and ideal values were by tradition excluded.

Realism, for its part, necessitated something else. The classical rule of the separation of styles, which became influential in the sixteenth century, stipulated in practice that everything pertaining to everyday life–social classes and occupations, the common events of life in real places actually named and described–had to be written in the 'low style', which meant that in theory it could not be treated on any level except the comic. We are expected to laugh at the astuteness the young protagonist of *Lazarillo de Tormes* has to develop in order to circumvent the difficulties life puts in his way; we laugh, too, at the cynical or extravagant characters with whom he is associated. This is true of all picaresque novels in varying degrees. Comic characters and wily ingenuity become conventions of the *genre* because realistic writing was not considered appropriate in any other way. In theory, this presupposed nar-. row boundaries for realism, since the comic excluded any serious treatment of a serious problem. In point of fact, in modern times the humorous elements in the novels have seemed to militate against, or belie, the serious intentions professed by their authors, and this apparent incongruity has led to the confusions described at the beginning of this chapter. Thus one critic asserts that *La vida del buscón* cannot be a picaresque novel because it is a 'moral tale', while another asserts that it does not have any moral implications because it is a humorous, witty work.[48] Another authority maintains that *Moll Flanders* is not a picaresque novel because it is not a comic work but, on the contrary, 'a serious study of the effects of heredity and environment in the making of criminals'.[49] As we shall see, what *El buscón* actually demonstrates, and demonstrates triumphantly, is that a work can both be witty and show a serious interest in delinquency. For what most modern critics have not realised is that the best of the Spanish picaresque novelists were engaged, as was Cervantes in *Don Quixote*,[50] in breaking down the barrier between the comic and the serious. This they did because they, and Cervantes also, were products of a culture that demanded that literature be both truthful and morally responsible.

The relation of realism to the comic and the ways in which, through the centuries, realistic subjects could be treated seriously, are the theme of Auerbach's remarkable book *Mimesis*.[51] *Don Quixote* has a chapter to itself but the Spanish picaresque novels are never mentioned. In his Epilogue, Auerbach regrets that he was not able to study the Spanish Golden Age more extensively, but in the work itself this literature is dismissed as 'not particularly important' in the history of 'the literary conquest of modern reality'. The reason for this is the often stated but not really well-founded assertion that this literature presents passions and conflicts but no problems, no riddles demanding solution, and no questioning of the immutable order of the world and society. For Auerbach the full emancipation of realism from the comic comes in modern times when the existence of society is seen to pose problems which require the exploration of the motive forces within it. In antiquity, realistic literature, at its best, might pose a problem in ethics, but the problem is one for the individual only, since the ethical question is more concerned with the individual members of society than with the social whole; and this is also true of the Spanish Golden Age.[52] Auerbach traces this particular emancipation magnificently, but it is surely an arbitrary delimitation of significant realism. It is not only in this direction that the barrier between the comic and the serious can be broken down. The Spanish picaresque novels do not widen the scope of realism by seeing society as 'problematic' or by acquiring an awareness of history; but the two best, at least, do explore reality by building up an existential picture of an individual who, under social and psychological influences to which he has been subject from childhood, chooses a certain pattern of experience in which to realize himself in action, and is moulded by it. *Don Quixote*, in a different psychological and social context, does this also. Nothing like this had been achieved in any earlier novel, for the life-story of an Amadis, whatever else it might have been, was not existential. Such a development cannot rightly be excluded from the history of the conquest of reality in European literature.[53]

2

The Delinquent Emerges

ALTHOUGH *Lazarillo de Tormes* should be kept historically and thematically distinct from the picaresque *genre* proper, it must be given its due as the precursor. It was this, among other things, in the way it demonstrated that a work could be amusing and witty and yet show a serious social interest. This is the only aspect that bears on the treatment of delinquency in literature.[1]

The Prologue states the intended purpose of the story. The rich, it says, have no merit if they lead good lives, because life is made easy for them by the inheritance of every social advantage. With the poor, however, it is different: they, indeed, are meritorious if, starting with no advantage of any kind, they manage to win for themselves a respectable social position and economic security. The boy, Lázaro, illustrates the merit due to the self-made man. His origins are the most inauspicious possible. His family background is a sordid one of immorality and of a poverty for which thieving is the only remedy. As his mother casts him out into the world at an age when human beings are still in need of the security of family life, she tells him, as her parting advice, that now that he is on his own he must try to be good. This is the only advice she can give him, but it is of course inconsistent with his up-bringing. The boy has never known goodness, only the struggle on the mother's part, and that of her paramour, to keep alive by dishonest means. Only by education and good example can a boy learn to be good. His moving now from master to master is the education he receives from life. One after the other drives home two lessons: first, that no help is to be obtained from one's fellow-men and that the only course to pursue is selfishly to look after one's own interests; and secondly, that what rules in society is hypocrisy, that the profession of religion, charity, or the show of honour and respectability, are cloaks covering cruelty, avarice, pride, and fraud.

In order to make his way in the world—in order to keep alive at all—Lázaro must become what each of his masters is—a hypocrite. He first becomes this when he is forced to resort to tricks and stratagems which must be concealed; life for him is not above-board. But unlike the real picaroons who come later, Lázaro does not develop criminal instincts, for the author's intention is not to lead him into delinquency but to the summit of hypocrisy; this he reaches when he marries the mistress of an Archpriest who gives Lázaro certain economic benefits in exchange for the advantage of being able to continue the liaison under social cover. Lázaro, having learnt where his interests lie, is prepared to counter gossip by swearing on the Consecrated Host that his wife is an honest woman. In this way he attains to the security and respectability that his birth made it necessary for him to achieve by his own merits. The poor, who can rise only by means of a dependence on their fellow-men, will do so by learning that respectability and prosperity are masks for complacent self-dishonour. This is a judgement that depends for its irony on a concern for moral values in a socio-economic setting; and this, in 1554, was something quite new in the novel.

The strongest satire in *Lazarillo* is directed against hypocritical religious observance, which is why the novel fits into the environment of religious reform. Similar satire occurs later in Cervantes's short story *Rinconete y Cortadillo*, written before 1604 and thus contemporaneous with the rise of the picaresque *genre*, into which it is Cervantes's only venture. The gang of the thieves and pickpockets of Seville, which he portrays, is organized along the lines of a religious confraternity. Their consciences do not prick them because they do not consider their thieving incompatible with the observance of religion. They attend church and say their prayers regularly; they put aside part of their ill-gotten gains as an offering for the Church, and they never steal on Fridays. It is true that they also avoid such religious practices as might conflict with their profession: they never go to confess their sins, because they would then be required to restore their stolen goods before being given absolution. Similarly, they are not troubled by the thought that they may be excommunicated, because they stay away from church on the days when the decrees of excommunication are read from the pulpits. There is something engaging about the naïve self-confidence these thieves have that they are regulating their lives according to religious standards and gaining spiritual merit by their pious good works; but the humorous irony has, of course, a serious intention. The Seville criminals are able to persuade themselves that their lives are upright and religious, because religion for them means merely the external forms of devotional practice with nothing of the inner spirit. Religion in them has become superstition, a danger to which all institutional religion is liable.

Because it leads us into a *milieu* of delinquency this Exemplary Novel is a picaresque story in a way that *Lazarillo* is not; but in tone and satirical intention it is in the line of *Lazarillo* and still far removed from the deeper preoccupation with delinquency that the picaresque *genre* will reveal. For Cervantes shows only one aspect of delinquency—the most naïve and humorous aspect—and shows it as a self-subsisting world, already formed and static; it is a limited manifestation of delinquent psychology rather than an exploration of it. His thieves are caught in the trap and are happy in it; he does not try or want to tell us either how they came to be ensnared or how they could struggle to escape. *Guzmán de Alfarache* of Mateo Alemán does precisely this; it attempts to portray, for the first time in novelistic form, the individual experience of delinquency in its full range. It does this within the context of religious doctrine and experience, that of temptation, sin, and repentance.

¶ Enrique Moreno Báez has been the first to see this novel as serving the religious ends of the Counter-Reformation and mirroring the theological preoccupations of its age.[2] I find the main lines of his thesis fully convincing, but not all critics have shared this opinion. Alberto del Monte maintains[3] that Moreno's thesis has been definitively refuted by J.A. van Praag[4]; but this refutation does not bear examination. It is apparently based on a questionable assumption: that no man of Jewish descent could really be a convinced Christian in the Spain of 1600. Taking this for granted, van Praag gives a long list of quotations from the novel, all of which are alleged to show a mocking, sarcastic or cynical attitude to Catholic doctrines and practices. These interpretations are, however, due to unfamiliarity with Catholic usage and tradition, to disregard of the non-literal character of many Spanish idioms, to disregard of the context and to a failure to distinguish cases where the author speaks 'in character' from those where he speaks in person. Proof of these assertions will be found in an appendix.

I have no wish to imply that Alemán, who was of Jewish descent on both his father's and his mother's side, did not have much to suffer on this account, psychologically and socially, or that he did not feel much bitterness and resentment. Nor do I wish to deny that Alemán could have been a sceptical or unconvinced Christian in his heart of hearts; all I maintain is that, if he was, he succeeded in hiding the fact so well that nobody suspected it for 300 years until his *converso* ancestry was discovered. He clearly *intended* to write an orthodox work, to contribute (as we now see it) to Counter-Reformation literature, and his book was passed by ecclesiastical censors in an age when the Inquisition was vigilant to protect both the purity and dignity of the Faith, and when inquisitors and censors were well trained to do their job. They were to object to some of Quevedo's jokes and expressions as being irreverent, but not one objected to any of the expressions of Alemán listed by van Praag. Further, the book has been read for four centuries and a half by Spanish Catholics, not one of whom has ever objected to irreverence or blasphemy in it. The weight of evidence is overwhelmingly on Moreno's side, reinforced by the fact that Alemán's only other major work is a Life of St Anthony of Padua,[5] which was praised by two censors for the orthodoxy of its doctrine and which earned from Lope de Vega a laudatory poem. In this eulogy he says that if St Anthony is another Christ, Mateo Alemán is another Matthew, a writer whose pen wings its way upwards, carrying him to heaven.[6]

None-the-less, even when the orthodoxy of *Guzmán de Alfarache* has not been called in question, its religious sincerity has often been denied. This begins with the French seventeenth- and eighteenth-century translators and is ultimately due to the novel's structure, which needs to be first discussed. A whole series of didactic digressions are interpolated into the fictional narrative. The obvious reason for this is that Alemán wanted the novel to be a doctrinal one, to have a 'thesis', and perhaps he could not think of a way of making his doctrine emerge from his narrative plot; he thus fell back on the religious writings like *La conversión de la Magdalena* or, no doubt, on the sermons that were preached every Sunday.[7] But it is also probable that discursiveness was ingrained in Alemán's temperament. Moreno has pointed out how often he makes Guzmán refer with alarm to his own prolixity in case he is boring the reader.[8] *San Antonio de Padua* offers a much more interesting example of this self-consciousness. In the Prologue Alemán states that a historian should write history bare of irrelevancies and clothed in truth. He himself has fulfilled the second requirement but not the first, because the lives of saints must serve as examples to us and this requires that they be glossed with 'moralities' and 'allegories' from which the reader can derive profit.[9] It would follow, therefore, that since a picaroon's life is also exemplary (in the opposite way), it deserves or requires the same treatment. The opening chapters of *San Antonio* deal with the history of Lisbon; at the beginning of the fourth, Alemán, becoming perturbed at the possible criticism that all this has nothing to do with the saint, justifies himself by saying that it is a habit of his in his writings, and he does not think it a bad one, to pursue the interesting aspects of the topics that come into his mind, thus following the road as it opens up before him. Everything that is good and interesting in itself always has a relevance somewhere.[10] In this particular case, praise of Lisbon and Portugal redounds to the glory of St Anthony, for he was born there.[11] Thus Alemán proceeds with his history and pious legends, even including a chapter that is not unlike a tourist's guide to the city, and does not reach the saint's birth until the sixth chapter.

If, then, Alemán was a born rambler, he would not have been troubled, as Cervantes always was, by any laws of composition; it would never have occurred to him that his plot and the thesis he wished it to carry could or should be fused together. We are less particular about literary form than our teachers used to be, and our pupils are even less particular than we are. Although our age has little sympathy with overt didacticism, the dualistic structure of *Guzmán de Alfarache* need not, *qua* structure, be the stumbling-block it once was. We can concede that it is an artistic defect but not that it thereby lessens the significance of the work. What is a stumbling-block, however, is the difference of tone between the digressions and the narrative. Sometimes the former inveigh loudly against vices which the latter describes with a certain degree of delectation.[12] Those who have objected to this have not taken into account that Alemán was compelled, by the 'low style' in which his narrative had to be written, to amuse his readers; he had to make Guzmán's skill as a thief diverting through its ingenuity. The problem does not lie in the existence of the delectation itself, but in the existence of the religious and ethical doctrine that accompanies it; because the two, it is alleged, are incompatible, the second should not be there.[13] The novel has thus been persistently criticized for attempting to cover up in hypocritical moralizing a relish for unsavoury delinquency. This criticism can, however, be answered, or at least an explanation can be given for what is criticized. To a considerable extent, differences of religious traditions must colour the spectacles of the readers. In trying to be objective I do not want to appear to suggest either that the Catholic attitude to sin is complacent or that the Protestant attitude is priggish; but there is a difference that is probably instinctive and that is based on the presence or absence of the confessional. On the one hand there is the habit of viewing sins as things to be disclosed, on the other that of viewing them as things to be concealed; in the latter case there can be an embarrassment and a shame at disclosure which can be absent in the former, where shame will be felt more at concealment. The penitent Guzmán, a Catholic, has the spiritual and psychological compulsion to tell his sins, and he calls his story of his life a 'general confession'.[14] The reader thus sits, as it were, in the priest's place, not to judge, still less to condemn sanctimoniously, for it is the penitent who condemns himself, but to give as the equivalent of absolution the gift of sympathy and understanding; for the reader is, or should be, himself involved in the confession since, in the framework in which it is set by Alemán, it is the confession not so much of an individual delinquent as of delinquent humanity.

Those who accuse Alemán of a hypocritical dualism should, in justice, bear in mind that different spiritualities form different habits. In any case, his metaphor of the confessional is helpful in discussing the criticism itself. A priest's task in listening to the confessions of penitents cannot be an agreeable one, but he does it out of duty. Alemán's difficulty in obtaining from his readers absolution for his protagonist, the symbol of delinquent humanity, is that they are not obliged to listen to him out of duty; they will listen to the end only if they are attracted in the way proper to imaginative literature, by what is said and the way it is said. Since this is literature in the 'low style', Alemán is caught in the horns of a dilemma: he must 'amuse' by making his delinquent recount his misdeeds with a certain delectation, yet these are misdeeds of which much later, at the time of writing, he had repented. The delectation takes the form either of satisfaction at his cleverness or of cynical irony, the tone of which is sometimes unpleasant. Yet this is also essential from the point of view of characterization, for psychological plausibility requires the author to convey something of the attractiveness of sin in general–the nature, that is to say, of temptation–and the particular satisfaction his character gets, or thinks it gets, from committing sin. Because the character is not psychotic but an ordinary man, the truthful and honest account of how he falls deeper into sin cannot but be a temptation to anyone who reads it to enjoy transgression in imagination. This is why Alemán's moralizing digressions are so frequent and so forceful. This dualism is not the best solution to the problem of conveying both the tempting and the repellent aspects of sin, but it is an honest solution, not a hypocritical one. And it was only by facing the problem at all that a novel could, within a religious culture, be a serious attempt to study delinquency.

To make matters still worse for Alemán, he was handicapped by his use of autobiographical form. In this, it is not likely that he was influenced only by *Lazarillo de Tormes*, for the form has, of course, a long and important tradition in religious literature, beginning with the *Confessions* of St Augustine. The difficulty presented by this form of narration is that the career of the delinquent is recounted by him with the thoughts and feelings he had while experiencing these events, yet it is in fact being narrated by someone who has undergone a religious conversion. Alemán cannot or will not disclose at the beginning the fact of the future conversion in order not to mar the ascent to the climax by breaking novelistic suspense. Right from the start he discloses that it is a galley slave who is writing his life-story; but the concealment that Guzmán is also a converted penitent lands him into difficulties, for while the moralizing digressions are appropriate in the mouth of such a man, the reader knows him only as the delinquent he is describing. As early as the second chapter Guzmán is made to point out how inappropriate are moral sentiments in his mouth, without his being able to disclose that it is a repentant and not a hardened sinner who is talking. This helps to create the impression of hypocrisy, not only by the disparity of tone but by the ease with which many critics have confused the narrator's two voices, the one belonging to the time of narrating, the other belonging to the time of the action. It is not really difficult to know when the author is speaking in person and when in character, but Alemán did not foresee how much help many of his readers and even of his critics would none-the-less need.

All this indicates that *Guzmán de Alfarache* is not an easy, straightforward book; it has, on the contrary, a complicated structure arising from a tension between content and form, between two different time sequences, and between two different levels of experience. This makes it, as regards its form, a much more modern work for us than it could have been for our predecessors one or more generations ago. Add to the interest of this tension the fact that it is written in a magnificent style, nervous and taut, and one has the framework for a significant novel. Its much-maligned dualism of structure is something that need no longer repel (a not dissimilar structure, incidentally, has never repelled in *Moby Dick*). The novel should be accepted as, on the one hand, the story of an individual

---

[3.] Mateo Alemán. From the first edition (1599) of the First Part of *Guzmán de Alfarache*.

In insidijs non est prudentia

Ga:g: Bouttat. inven: et sculp.

human life, and, on the other hand, as a series of comments on the spiritual and moral values in which human lives are set. By itself the story or narrative is a valid novel; within the setting of the comments it is something more—a serious attempt to focus the problem of delinquency.

The narrative, in outline, is as follows. Setting out as a youth to make his fortune, with a family life behind him that was morally sordid, Guzmán begins by gambling and becomes a petty thief. Emigrating to Italy he becomes a sham beggar in Rome; by painting sores on his legs he lives deceitfully on charity.[15] Taken into the household of a Cardinal who has pity on him, Guzmán has the chance of settling down to a life of honest service with a kind master, but he rejects it and exploits the Cardinal's kindness in order to steal from him. Losing his post, he gradually becomes a thief on a large scale, amasses a lot of money and settles down in Madrid as a wealthy merchant, taking advantage of every possible loophole in the law to live by financial swindling. Eventually he is found out and his whole prosperity collapses. Faced with the necessity of starting anew, he decides to ensure a livelihood by becoming a priest, and proceeds to the university to embark on his studies prior to ordination. What begins as a shameless and cynical self-interest becomes another chance of a turning-point: he begins to take his studies seriously, and slowly becomes a reformed character; he might have become to some extent sincere in his vocation, but temptation comes in the shape of a woman with whom he falls madly in love. Despite his better nature and the advice of all his teachers, he gives up his student's life to marry her. Deeper degradation follows when he finds that his wife is not an honest woman, and he comes to live off her prostitution, which he furthers himself. Eventually his wife abandons him, and he determines to

---

[4.] 'Guzmán is received into the household of a Cardinal who takes pity on him' (p. 37). From the Verdussen (Antwerp 1681) edition of *Guzmán de Alfarache*.

swindle by posing as a saint. He steals a bag of money and takes it to a priest, saying he has found it but, although he is destitute, does not want to keep it; will the priest announce the find from the pulpit so that the owner can claim it? Deeply impressed with this honesty, the priest praises him so warmly in his sermon that Guzmán gains the reputation of being a saint, which he proceeds to exploit by stealing from the charitable people who come forward to help him. Found out, he is brought to trial and sentenced to punishment as a galley-slave. Here, in the depths both of moral degradation and physical misery, the lowest type of social outcast, he undergoes a moral and spiritual conversion. And the novel ends; a promised Third Part was never written.[16]

Before I discuss the psychological motivation and plausibility of the final conversion, let me first briefly explain the thesis behind this narrative. In this comprehensive panorama of society there is an unchanging emphasis on the corruption of men—all are callous, selfish, each is out for himself at the expense of his neighbour. And this is not due to the times, not due, that is, to specific historical conditions. Alemán's satire is not limited to his age and country. Strictly speaking it is not satire at all, because it is a universal judgement on human nature. The evil of life is not due to political, economic or social conditions that can be reformed, thereby removing the evil. The evil is something inherent in human nature. Institutions change, men remain the same. The delinquent protagonist is no exception to the general run of humanity. The spotlight is focused on him because he is the representative of mankind. On this universalized plane the work seeks to establish certain theological propositions, which Moreno Báez was the first to detect.

The general pessimism of the book, the equality of all men in sin, is the first proposition: namely, Original Sin. The fundamental point of departure for the study of human nature is not its potential nobility but its potential depravity. Yet, also fundamental is the second proposition: that all men are equally capable of salvation. To proceed from the one proposition to the other is a huge theological jump. This is bridged by the development of the delinquent's character and career in which three other moral and theological propositions are both implicit in the episodes of the narrative and explicit in the digressions. First, man is free to choose between good and evil; there is no determinism, and proneness to passion does not destroy responsibility. Secondly, all things are governed by Providence; nothing therefore happens to a man that he cannot utilize for his own good. God, wishing the salvation of all men, gives to each the means if men realize how to accept, bear, and profit from it. Thirdly, man can therefore, of his own free will, co-operate with Divine Grace to make his salvation effective.

There seems to me to be more in the narrative plot to support this interpretation than Moreno himself detected. Let us consider, for instance, the first two chapters. This is the section of the work that leaves the nastiest taste in the mouth; here it would seem that Guzmán really does gloat on exposing the shamelessness of both his parents. Many of the critics who are hostile to the moral tone of the book may well have allowed their reactions to be permanently coloured by this opening. This apparent relish at disclosure after disclosure is furthermore improbable. If one's parents are monsters of iniquity, one would have to be utterly degraded to take pleasure in disclosing the fact; it is an attitude which is therefore more appropriate to the unrepentant picaroon than to the spiritually regenerate convert. But the very improbability of this situation, together with the extraordinarily exaggerated list of the parents' vices points to the need for a different focus.

There is scarcely a sin, either against God or man, which Guzmán does not impute to his father. He was a thief, a swindler, a renegade, a man who deserted his wife after stealing her fortune, and one who bribed the ministers of the law. As if this were not enough, Guzmán proceeds to hint that his father was also a homosexual without at the same time ceasing to run after women; this imputation is absolutely unnecessary unless it is the case that Alemán wants to establish at the start that Guzmán's father was guilty of every enormity. As for the mother, she was an adulteress, in fact almost a common prostitute; but this is nothing compared to her own mother, whose behaviour was so promiscuous that she could give her daughter no idea who her father might really have been. The female line in Guzmán's ancestry was depraved; when this is added to the fact that the father was guilty of every sin, we must conclude Alemán is not painting a realistic picture of an ancestry, since it is much too exaggerated for that, but a symbolic picture. Guzmán has no ancestry at all to be proud of, no family honour to give him a sense of self-respect; his whole stock is tainted. This is clearly a symbol of Original Sin, which is the taint of dishonour in the whole human race, the root from which all human sinfulness grows. The implication is that when any man looks back on his ancestry, on humanity as a whole, there is nothing he can be proud of; so Alemán loads every sin, gratuitously, upon the back of Guzmán's father in order to make him a universal representative of humanity, not an individual. Thus Guzmán comments: 'You see here...that [since] the whole current [runs] with a troubled water, my father followed along with the stream and did as others did, and was not the sole and only offender...God lend us his helping hand, that we may not fall into other the like miseries: for all of us, even the best of us, we are but men.'[17] By itself this comment is a clear enough reference to Original Sin, and this must serve as my illustration of the novel's dual structure; the comment is the universal context within which the particular narrative is to be interpreted: there is all the time a non-narrative background against which much of the realism of the narrative can take on a symbolic value.

There is thus an indication at the start that Guzmán's passage through the world may well be symbolical of mankind's spiritual odyssey. While there is in his development nothing of the exaggeration with which he described his parents, the details with which the development is presented often point to something beyond themselves. One further example can show how a religious interpretation follows naturally out of the narrative itself. Guzmán's first experience of life after leaving home is that it is not a bed of roses: he is given bad food, he is bitten by fleas, he is mistaken for a thief and robbed of his cloak. Thus, at the beginning of Book ii of Part I, he is entirely alone in the world, entirely disillusioned, and without a cloak (that is, without the status of a gentleman) –in short, with nothing he can rely on to be respected by others. The situation, as described, is natural; but it can, without any distortion whatever, be seen as symbolical of the natural man without grace–man left to his own resources in a world that, by nature, is hostile or at least unwelcoming. In this lonely and disillusioned state the effects of Original Sin begin to operate as a natural inclination to slide into wrong-doing, a sort of inertia, a disinclination to take any positive steps to impose self-discipline.[18] This is how Guzmán drifts into the life of a street-urchin. At this point he feels the call of 'this glorious freedom', whose praises he sings. It is the glory of being his own master, subject to no law, convention or re-straint; it is the appeal of anarchy, the call of delinquency; so that in due course Guzmán finds it less irksome, and therefore 'freer', to stay a beggar than to use his hoarded alms to buy decent clothes and return to the constraints of society. If the reader is looking at all this with religious eyes, then the way that Guzmán joins the brotherhood of the professional beggars in Rome appears as a travesty of profession into a religious order, with the taking of vows, the acceptance of asceticism (through sloth), the obedience to a Master General and the renunciation of the pomp and vanity of the world by turning his back on discipline and honour.[19] Although he will be momentarily rescued from this life, against his will, by the charity of the Cardinal, in whose service he will suffer the hardship of work and will hanker after the flesh-pots of beggary, his joining the brotherhood is the training for the life of delin-quency, namely the thieving and swindling on which he will embark in order to assert his cleverness and remain socially free by possessing a wealth that he has not needed to work for.

In addition to opening into this kind of symbolism, the novel has a clear structural pattern. The story of the delinquent is one of slow decline, but it is punctuated by a regularly recurring feature, taking two forms: first, Guzmán is constantly offered the opportunity of a different kind of livelihood (of which the two crucial instances are service in the Cardinal's house and later his studies at the University); and secondly, he is subject, from time to time, to pangs of conscience. Moreno Báez is clearly right in seeing this structural pattern as denoting, on the doctrinal level, the natural movement towards evil, counteracted by divine grace offering men all the time the means of ultimate salvation. The plot of *Guzmán de Alfarache* has certainly not got the loose formlessness that is supposed to characterize the Spanish examples of the picaresque novel.

Anyone who knows what theological interests are and who is tolerant enough to allow a seventeenth-century novelist to have them, cannot fail to be convinced by the general interpretation of this novel by Moreno Báez, despite the strong tradition, which goes back to Chandler, against any religious interpretation. Those who do not know what these interests are, or who disapprove of a novelist being so 'committed' as to promulgate them in his work, will not be prepared to accept *Guzmán de Alfarache* as a significant work of literature; but this is less a question of interpretation than of personal taste. Alemán does, of course, select his material to make his theological points, but he does not distort it. All the way through, the novel is a convincing presentation of a human character and his environment. Guzmán is highly intelligent; he also has a conscience. He sins with his eyes open, and always against his better nature. He is a tormented or tragic character, divided against himself; his reason pulls him one way, his will another; and his reason cannot control his will. He never loses his religious faith, but until the end this is only an intellectual conviction, never an emotional or passionate one—and in Guzmán the will is pulled all the time by the emotions. He can only become a unified personality when his emotions feel to be good that which his reason and his conscience recognize to be so. This unification comes when, as a galley-slave, he feels in his very bones the emptiness that vice has brought him. He experiences then an emotional revulsion against his whole life, which combines with the intellectual revulsion. It is no longer just an abstract awareness of the good but a concrete one, as a result of experiencing in the depths of his being the negativeness of evil. In this way, although his life has been a steady moral and social decline, it has also been in some sense a spiritual rise. This he expresses in a very striking, and indeed profound, paradox:

> And as I was thinking and considering on these things,
> I said one night with myself: Guzmán, thou seest here
> the top of that mountain of miseries, whereunto thy
> filthy sensuality has brought thee: now art thou come
> to the highest part of it, and must either make a speedy
> leap down to the bottomless pit of hell, or which thou
> mayest more easily do, by lifting up thy arms, take hold
> on Heaven.[20]

It is the summit and not the abyss of misery because, all complacency being now impossible and freedom having absolutely nothing to offer, he can accept spiritual regeneration with his will. Since the world is no longer an object that it is possible to love, his will no longer sets up a barrier to his intellect and conscience.[21] The constancy of his conversion is subjected to immediate and severe trials, to which he does not succumb. The novel has a moving end. Wrongly accused of having stolen a jewelled hat-band that has been lost, he is flogged and tortured in order to be made to confess; not only does he bear his suffering with fortitude, but he gains at last the full stature of his human dignity when he sorrows more for the inhumanity of his fellows than for himself: 'And the greatest grief that I did feel in these my miseries, was not so much for the pain which I did endure, nor for the false witness that was given against me, as that all of them should have believed I deserved this punishment and took no pity on me.'[22] It is on this deep note that the first picaresque novel closes—the note of pity for a humanity that knows no pity.

Many modern readers may be disturbed by the continuation of the story: Guzmán's fellow-slaves try to enlist his help in a conspiracy to seize the ship, but he, determined never to sin again, denounces the conspiracy to the captain, as a result of which the ringleaders are executed and Guzmán rewarded for his loyalty by being given the freedom of the ship, pending the pardon that is petitioned for him. This violates our instincts of fair play; apart from which we are nowadays also conditioned to sympathy with most insurrections, especially those of slaves. The seventeenth century, however, had a horror of insurrections, and Guzmán's denunciation of this one was for Alemán and his contemporary readers the sign of his turning away from delinquency by submission to discipline, order, and justice. The manner of Guzmán's release ought not, therefore, to affect our judgement of his prior repentance. The conversion itself is so movingly presented that it is impossible, if one has read the whole work properly, to doubt its sincerity. Yet those critics who dismiss it as hypocritical are more numerous than those who accept it as genuine.[23] Perhaps we may grow out of this, as we have grown out of the once almost universal disapproval of Cervantes for bringing Don Quixote to repentance on his death-bed. Non-Hispanists, when referring to Alemán's novel in connexion with French and English picaresque novels, generally either disregard the conversion or imply that it never happened; but they, as will be seen later, have an excuse.

Guzmán de Alfarache has not the formal unity that would satisfy the purist, but it has a complex structure that can fascinate the critic and reader whose interests are less superficial. It does not offer easy reading, and although it has elements of comedy, it is not, taken as a whole, entertaining in any agreeable sense; yet it is a novel that can shake the complacency of any reader who does not refuse to accept its premises as tenable. Whether one accepts or rejects the validity of its 'thesis', there should be no denying that Alemán chose delinquency as subject-matter for a novel because it provided scope for an intelligent and earnest attempt to investigate the nature of moral evil.

The same, however, cannot be said for all its successors. Between Alemán's First and Second Parts there appeared in 1602 an apocryphal Second Part under the name Mateo Luján de Saavedra, a pseudonym for a Valencian lawyer called Juan Martí. In his true Second Part, Alemán says that he was compelled by Martí to scrap what he had written and compose another continuation. Martí must have had access to his manuscript or known of Alemán's intentions, but despite this his continuation is a clumsy and, on the whole, rather boring work which need not detain us, for it makes no new contribution to the literary treatment of picaresque material; on the contrary it greatly lowers the tension, not only by turning the protagonist into a very commonplace character but by making his misdemeanours very minor affairs, until at the end he waylays men in the streets at night to steal their cloaks. He embarks on this robbery in order to obtain money to enjoy the favours of an actress, and for it he is sentenced to the galleys; the novel comes to an end as he is marched off to the port, promising a Third Part with the account of how he later escaped. In Alemán, life as a galley-slave is an organic part of a consistent character development; in Martí, it is out of keeping with what has gone before, an artificial ending required to fulfil what Alemán had announced in the First Part.

¶ *Guzmán de Alfarache* and its two Second Parts immediately established the new genre with its conventions of form, character and plot. These made for much less uniformity than has commonly been supposed, and the next novel is as different from *Guzmán* as it could possibly be. This is *La pícara Justina*, the first of the line of female rogues. It appeared in 1605, but must have gone to press before the Second Part of *Guzmán* was published.[24]

Histories of Spanish literature usually call this novel a 'curious' work. For Menéndez Pelayo it was 'extravagant, obscure, tedious' and a 'monument of bad taste.'[25] The fact that it did deserve this judgement by the standards of his time helped to disparage the Spanish exponents of the picaresque *genre* in general. The novel has also been constantly condemned as a particularly crude attempt to give a moral colour to a completely amoral story. The only saving grace it found, until recently, was its style, which is a treasure-house of the language of burlesque, a riot of verbosity in which popular speech is given an exuberant ornamentation by being overladen with the language of polite literature. The tone is low, frivolous, often crude, although with a certain robust vivacity, and as a picaresque story it is certainly boring. None-the-less, as Marcel Bataillon has now begun to show, the work is too intelligent to be thus lightly dismissed; it stems from the *entourage* of Rodrigo Calderón, the favourite of the Duke of Lerma, the chief minister of Philip III, and its burlesque facetiousness cloaks an ironical vision of many aspects of contemporary life. Bataillon argues that it was in fact written to amuse the high society of the capital by the way it disguised allusions to events, persons and places, and he has begun with remarkable perspicacity to offer the clues to the decipherment of these disguises, which contemporaries did not require but without which the work has been unintelligible for later generations. Although the work must, for these reasons, be considered to lie outside the series of picaresque novels, Bataillon none-the-less relates it closely to *Guzmán de Alfarache* as 'une riposte hilare à cette littérature de divertissement relativement grave'.[26] For my present purposes this judgement is crucial, and it is a possible expansion of it in one direction that I would put forward.

La pícara Justina was published under the name of Francisco López de Úbeda, who has been identified as a practising physician. But Cervantes's attack on the novel has been understood as implying that its author was a priest[27]; and Nicolás Antonio later in the seventeenth century recorded a tradition among the Dominicans that one of their number, Fray Andrés Pérez, had written the novel–not, as is commonly stated, when already a friar, but 'when his age made it permissible for him to rave like a madman', which implies before he joined the order.[28] Both the authorship of Fray Andrés Pérez and a presumed date of composition *c.* 1580 have been demolished by Bataillon. But it is none-the-less interesting that the Dominicans, an order of great intellectual standing, did not consider it slanderous to the memory of one of their brethren to father upon him the work of a 'madman'. There are, in fact, reasons why some ecclesiastics might conceivably have looked on the novel with less unfavourable eyes than an artist like Cervantes or a scholar like Antonio.

Úbeda claims in his preface that he had written it many years previously when a student at Alcalá and that now, after the appearance of *Guzmán de Alfarache*, he has amplified it and has determined to give it to the press. This is a face-saving device to pass off a work of levity as a juvenile production, for Bataillon has proved that the novel is closely connected with events in 1602–4. To me it also seems to depend, in conception and construction, on *Guzmán de Alfarache*: it emerges out of the same background, but in deliberate opposition to Alemán's belief that he could write a novel that would be both religious and realistic.

The prologue begins with praise of the learned and apostolic men who have attacked secular literature for flattering the senses but killing the soul. These men, says Úbeda, are the guardian angels of society trying to safeguard Christian children by preventing the knowledge or the memory of sin from entering the mind through the senses. The irony one here begins to suspect soon becomes more open. Such men, continues Úbeda, have not themselves been brought up on the literature of which they would deprive others. Their zeal, therefore, shows not only a great charity but also modesty and a spirit of mortification, because they are deliberately depriving themselves of the pleasures of literature – unless it is that their dedication to the things of the spirit makes them incapable of finding pleasure in anything the world approves of. This sly attack on the puritanical ecclesiastical conscience implicitly upholds the need for a secular literature; it is a plea that Cervantes, in a much gentler way, was to make explicit ten years later in the Prologue to his *Exemplary Novels*.[29]

After stating that the strenuous efforts of these zealous men have failed to prevent the publication of useless books, full of vanity and falsehood, Úbeda points out that this has had the unfortunate result that even books on religious subjects are now packed with inappropriate profane material, thus making what is professedly good more harmful than what is openly bad. It is not far-fetched to interpret this as a reference to *Guzmán de Alfarache*; it then becomes delightfully ironical that later ages should have reproached Alemán for introducing religious material into his picaresque story, when, in his own times, he was rebuked for introducing picaresque material into his religious tract.

All this shows, continues Úbeda, that there is no need to withhold his novel from publication; to ask him not to publish it would be tantamount to forbidding the preaching of sermons, because these attack vices which some of the faithful listening to them would not otherwise have known existed. In any case his book can safely see the light because he makes his didactic purpose explicit in the form of a moral appended to each chapter. Furthermore, publication of his book will also have the great advantage of preventing people from thinking that their own knowledge of evil is inaccessible to good and virtuous people, since it will show that the latter can acquire it by speculation and sound reasoning, without the need of experience. Here Úbeda is referring to himself, writing of low life without having lived it.

This subtle fooling cloaks two serious points. First, that to ban literature of entertainment will not keep the young innocent. Secondly, that it is impossible to expose the evil of sin without describing sins, and that nothing is therefore easier than to cloak an interest in sin in the garb of didactic moralizing; or conversely, that an author's good intentions do not prevent his being read out of morbid curiosity. Our contemporary literature being what it is, it would not be the pages of *Guzmán de Alfarache* that one would nowadays scan for the wrong reason; but in the Spain of 1600 things would have been different. These are, of course, problems that religion and education have always had to face, but the Reformation, and (especially in Spain) the Counter-Reformation, made them particularly acute. Úbeda's irony, in the context of his own picaresque novel, can be directed only against *Guzmán de Alfarache*, of which he would not yet have known the genuine Second Part. His suggestion, as I see it, is that Alemán is either hypocritical or misguided in following the demands of the ecclesiastics and thinking he can mix the spiritual and the profane to the advantage of the former. In the light of this, Úbeda's own method appears as a skit both on the religious writers, like Malón de Chaide, and on Alemán. First, his novel begins with a long introduction stressing that this is a *truthful* story and not full of falsehoods. It even contains the praise of Creation: just as the religious writers had sought to show that thorns on briars, stings on nettles, or poisonous creatures do not mar the essential goodness of nature, so Justina maintains that since everything that God has made is beautiful, the existence of picaroons, including herself, is justified. Secondly, the skit on *Guzmán* is implicit in the style and structure of the work. While Alemán's style is tense and earnest throughout, the dignified and clear style with which Úbeda writes his prologue gives way to the burlesque, sometimes even vulgar, floridity with which the picaresque part is written. Secondly, the actual narrative is only about a half of the whole, the other half being a series of digressions in the manner of Alemán, except that Úbeda's are about anything and everything and lose themselves eventually in meaningless frivolity. Thirdly, there are moralizing summaries at the end of each chapter. It is hard to believe that modern critics have thought these were seriously intended as sops to the censors; for Bataillon, because they are quite irrelevant to the stories from which they are supposed to be the extracted moral, they are further ways in which Úbeda pulls the legs of his gullible readers. While they are skits on moralistic literature in general, it seems to me that they can be considered skits on Alemán's digressions in particular, because they are usually extremely concise, in contrast to the verbosity of the body of the work and to the lengthiness of Alemán's moralizing; but above all because they are absurdly trite. Here, for instance, is one: 'The deceitfulness and the deceptions of the flesh are so subtle that rude, unlettered and ignorant persons are taken in by its tricks and its pleasures.'[30]

It can be maintained, therefore, that *La pícara Justina* is an implicit satire on the aims and structure of *Guzmán de Alfarache*, whose appearance was, as the Prologue states, the spur to its own publication. It seems to me that Úbeda (or the Dominican Andrés Pérez, who might conceivably have been one of the priests whom Úbeda states in his Prologue that he had consulted) honestly thought that *Guzmán* was not the way to write a work of entertainment combining pleasure and profit, that a low-life theme should not be treated seriously, and that the tone of realistic fiction should therefore be lowered. Úbeda's extraordinary language can be considered an intentional travesty of the 'low style' in order to counter the solemnity of Alemán. His aim was to make the new picaresque *genre* laughable, which is why his title-page does not offer the 'Life' of the heroine, but a 'Book of Entertainment' concerning her.

La pícara Justina therefore adds nothing to the exploration of delinquency, but it does add a new dimension to the *genre* – that of frivolous joking. This will be an important element in the literary decline of the picaresque novel in Spain. It also adds a new element to the literary material of delinquency by the creation of a female rogue, and thus helps in the long run to create Grimmelshausen's *Courasche* and Defoe's *Moll Flanders*. This will add a new sensationalism to the *genre*, but Úbeda himself has no such intention: his work is completely moral in the sense that nobody could possibly have been tempted to linger pruriently on any of its episodes.

The same is not true, however, of all Justina's female progeny. The next picaresque novel is, in fact, one that exploits, within the limits proper to polite literature, the particular type of sensationalism inherent in a female delinquent. This is *La hija de Celestina* (*The Daughter of Celestina*) by Alonso de Salas Barbadillo (1581–1635), published in 1612, and republished in 1614 in an expanded form with the title *La ingeniosa Elena* (*The Ingenious Helen*). The protagonist of a picaresque novel is now a *femme fatale*, a vivacious and beautiful woman whom men find irresistible, and who, not content with emptying their open purses, can steal their property by trickery and in the end murder her accomplice. This novel has not lacked admirers, but what they have admired seems to me only a slickness of style and technique, a pseudo-sophisticated tone and a gaiety that is very superficial. There is no attempt to probe delinquency, no explanation sought for the protagonist's behaviour other than the sparkle of her eyes. Her death on the gallows is only a conventional ending: there is no sense of guilt, or of tragedy, or of compassion. The work is, in short, at the very opposite pole from *Guzmán de Alfarache*, and this must be attributed directly to the influence of *La pícara Justina*.

The new *genre* has thus swayed between two extremes: in general, to use the literary language of the age, between profit without pleasure and pleasure without profit; in the particular sphere of realistic literature, between too much seriousness with too little comedy on the one hand, and no seriousness at all on the other. It was a question of finding the right tone in which to present delinquency as the subject of a novel. The right balance between the serious and the comic is not a problem for writers today, but it was a very real problem in the Spain of the early seventeenth century, and a twofold one: a moral problem and an aesthetic problem. Cervantes struck a beautiful balance in *Don Quixote*, but the picaresque sphere was more difficult. Alemán more than satisfied the moral requirements of his age, but not in the way proper to the literature of entertainment. Úbeda satisfied moral requirements only in a negative and therefore purely superficial way; in fact, his deliberate choice of jocularity and exuberance not only fails to satisfy the aesthetic sense, it also offends the moral sense. A search had to be made for a balanced solution.

3

Zenith and Nadir in Spain

THE first conscious attempt to find a middle-way solution to the problem of presenting delinquency in polite literature led the *genre* in a new direction. The next novel to appear was *Marcos de Obregón* (1618)[1] by the poet and musician Vicente Espinel (1550–1624), who, after an adventurous and peripatetic youth, took orders and became choirmaster of a Madrid church. His novel is to a considerable extent a genuine autobiography and it has proved possible to disentangle the fact from the fiction.[2] Espinel cast his memoirs in the form of fiction in order to make them more palatable, for his story links up with *Guzmán de Alfarache* in being the tale of a repentant sinner. He does not therefore eschew a moral purpose, but he is very conscious that he must steer a path between two extremes. Thus he writes in the Prologue:

> It was my aim to see whether I could succeed in writing in prose something that would be of profit to the commonwealth by giving both pleasure and instruction, following the precept of my master Horace; for some books have been published by men of great literary learning and reputation who cling so exclusively to doctrine that they have no opportunity for the mind to

recover breath and feel some pleasure; and other books
have appeared, so intent on giving pleasure by jests
and farcical tales, that after being stirred and sifted are
found to be so vain and futile, that nothing substantial
or profitable is left for the reader, and no credit is won
for their authors.[3]

These are the extremes of an exclusively religious literature on
the one hand and such works as *Justina* and *La hija de Celestina* on the other. It is legitimate to think that he included
Guzmán among the former, for it is certain that Espinel would
not have thought it fulfilled his own aim, which was to tune
the right note between the too tightly stretched string of doctrine and the too loosely stretched string of entertainment.
He is therefore consciously aiming at something different from
any picaresque novel published till then, and this he succeeded
in producing; for *Marcos de Obregón* is more discreet and restrained than its predecessors: the harshness and dark colours
of Alemán, the exuberant burlesque of Úbeda, the flippant
sensationalism of Salas Barbadillo—all these disappear. This
necessitates an alteration in the conventions. The work is
much more an adventure story than a picaresque novel, and
Marcos is not a picaroon or delinquent at all; he is an observer
of low life, of adventures that are neither crude nor cruel.
This detached position of the protagonist is achieved by a
device that, from the start, establishes the gentler tone.

In the case of *Guzmán* I emphasized the difficulty Alemán
had in avoiding incongruity between the tone of his comments
on life and the tone in which the misdeeds of his delinquent
had to be narrated, this incongruity arising from the novelistic
inadvisability of revealing at the beginning that the man who
was writing his life-story was a reformed character. Espinel's
technique is different: at the beginning we see Marcos as he
is when he is writing his story, a wise but not pedantic old
man, one who, without condoning wrong-doing, has a sympathetic understanding of human weakness. When he begins
his life story, we retain this impression of him all through the

adventures of his youth; he thus appears as a detached observer, because behind the narrating voice we sense the calm
experience of an old man. We see, too, a protagonist who is
usually able to right wrongs or to give picaroons a taste of
their own medicine, but who is never a picaroon himself. This
new tone and this new technique really remove the work from
the picaresque class, because there is no delinquency in the
protagonist and what there is in the environment is very much
watered down. In the endeavour to create profitable entertainment, Espinel, in fact, destroyed the special significance of the
genre. Instead of a psychological, spiritual, and social tension
between good and evil, he produced an agreeable enough, but
rather commonplace, balance that points directly to the neo-
classical world of Lesage, on whose *Gil Blas* he exercised the
greatest single influence.

A similar result is obtained in the religious sphere, by exactly the same change of narrative technique, in the next so-
called picaresque novel. This is *Alonso, mozo de muchos amos*
(*Alonso, Servant of Many Masters*)[4] by Jerónimo Alcalá
Yáñez (1563–1632), the First Part of which was published in
1624 and the Second in 1626. It is in dialogue form, Alonso
narrating his life in answer to questions and comments from
his interlocutor, who in Part I is the prior of the friary in
which Alonso is an unprofessed lay-brother, and in Part II
the parish priest of the district where Alonso is living as a
hermit. The device of first presenting the narrator as he is at
the end of the life he is describing has the same result as in
Marcos de Obregón, that of providing detachment from a world
that we know has been left behind. The fact that the narrator
is attached to a religious house, and is later a hermit, gives the
book a religious focus and aim throughout. Its main interest
is its return to the point of departure of the picaresque *genre*
with Alemán, and its attempt to do again what Úbeda had
said was impossible: to place this novelistic material in a religious setting. Alemán's method, as regards his narrative plot,
was the subtle one of keeping the religious doctrine implicit

symbolically in the tension of the picaresque action, gradually making it show through until it becomes fully explicit in the act of submission to the divine law, the reader being involved, like the protagonist, in the picaresque action and in the painful process of climbing the mountain of misery in order to reach up to heaven.

In *Alonso, mozo de muchos amos*, however, the method is much simpler, and is, in fact, entirely obvious. The world of religion is explicit from the very start as the goal of the human journey, and from this safe vantage point both protagonist and reader watch mankind's procession through the world without taking part. This non-involvement and sense of security from first to last robs the story of any tension, of any suffering or anguish. For this reason it is not to my mind a genuinely religious book, or at least not significantly so, whereas *Guzmán de Alfarache* is; for in the former, religion is an escapist refuge, at life's beginning so to speak, while in the latter it is the meaning to life that emerges at the end out of the existential agony of having to act by the mere fact of being free, of *not* being in a refuge. Alcalá's vantage-point of the religious house, and later of the hermitage, colours the narrative: there is an atmosphere of peacefulness, an air of innocence in the adventures, and the work is very chaste, not because there is any real apprehension of the ideal of purity but merely because the women who appear are generally ugly. From the point of view of this book, which is to see whether picaresque literature could come to grips with the problem of delinquency, *Alonso, mozo de muchos amos* is an evasion of the issue.

¶ None-the-less, despite these symptoms of decline, it is at this point, chronologically, that the *genre* reaches its zenith at the hands of a genius of the first order, Francisco de Quevedo Villegas (1580–1645), in the form of his only novel, *La vida del buscón*.[5] This appeared in 1626, but on the basis of a remark in the text indicating that Ostend is being besieged, it is generally thought to have been written in 1604, since the city was finally captured in September of that year. This would mean that Quevedo wrote it at the early age of twenty-four, which is very hard to believe even for a man of his genius, for the work has a depth of psychological insight and a mature control of a complex style beyond the capacity of a young man. A close comparison of its style with that of other satirical works of his whose dates of composition are known would not be likely, in my opinion, to point to a date much earlier than 1620.

The word *buscón*, which means 'thief' and 'swindler', has been variously rendered in translations of the novel as 'sharper', 'rascal', and (quite incorrectly) 'scavenger'. Although there are five different English translations[6] it must be emphasized that much of the work is untranslatable. For instance, the description of Cabra, the miserly schoolmaster, in cap. III contains the sentence *la nariz, entre Roma y Francia, porque se le había comido de unas bubas de resfriado, que aun no fueron de vicio, porque cuestan dinero*; which means, 'his nose [lay] between Rome and France, because it had been eaten away by sores from colds; they weren't even from vice, because those cost money.' *Roma* also means a flat or snub nose; venereal disease was called 'the French illness'; therefore, 'his nose lay between Rome and France....' The most recent translator renders this: 'His nose, which had once been a Roman one, had been worn flat by sores, from colds, but which one would have thought to come from the French disease except that that illness involves the price of a girl.'[7] The startling geographical witticism evaporates. Consider this sentence from the same paragraph: *Traía un bonete los días de sol, ratonado con mil gateras, y guarniciones de grasa*. The same translator has: 'On sunny days he wore a cap; it was riddled with holes and had a trimming of grease.' But *bonete* is the clerical biretta; it is also the bastion of a fortified wall (with protruding angles like the corners of a biretta); *ratonado* means riddled by mice, and the holes, *gateras*, are the openings in walls or roofs for cats to pass through, so that we have a momentary vision of cats and mice, chasing themselves in and out of the biretta; *guarniciones* does mean 'trimmings', but it also means 'garrison' and so connects with the 'bastion' of the biretta; it is garrisoned only by *grasa*, which in the sense of lard or bacon fat is suitable food for mice, who therefore 'riddle' it, but which in the sense of grease stains means that the wearer's unwashed head transfers to the biretta its only 'trimmings'. The novel is full of this complex playing on words, brilliantly sustained, which is either lost or falls flat in translation. For virtuosity of language, Quevedo has no equal in Spanish literature.

El buscón is essentially, in intention and execution, a humorous work. It represents the culmination, in the picaresque novel, of the 'low' or comic style, doing to perfection what Úbeda had thought was demanded by the subject-matter. But, in contrast to *La pícara Justina*, Quevedo's humour is not inappropriate to, or incompatible with, a serious interest in delinquency, for it is not festive or sprightly but pungent and sardonic; rather than humour proper, it is wit of a sharp-pointed kind. It stretches and distorts realism into caricature, creating a grotesque world of surrealist fancy. When the two boys were carried home after being starved at Cabra's boarding-school, they were so emaciated that 'spies' had to be brought to search for their eyes 'all over their faces'; the dust had to be removed from inside their mouths with foxtail brushes as if they were the easily damaged statues on the retables of altars; the doctors forbade anyone to speak in more than a whisper in their bedroom so that the words should not echo in their hollow stomachs; their cheeks had become so wrinkled through lack of chewing that each day the inside of their mouths had to be slowly moulded back into shape with pestles.[8] Isolated examples like this would suggest an extravaganza for its own sake, but when wit and plot are interrelated and the novel looked at as a whole, it becomes clear that this world is made grotesque in order to reveal the distortions and unreality of human social life in the self-conceit and hypocrisy of men.

Thus, the grotesque description of the miserly Cabra concludes with the outward signs of his priesthood. First his biretta already referred to, then his cassock: this is called 'miraculous'. We think of Christ's garment which healed the woman who touched it and of Christ as the exemplar of the priestly life, but this first impression is immediately shattered. The cassock is miraculous because 'you couldn't tell what colour it was. Some, seeing it so threadbare, thought it was made of frogskin; others said that it was an illusion; close by it seemed black, from afar bluish; he wore it without a girdle.' In the literature of the time the sky was sometimes called a falsehood because its blue colour is illusory; the cassock, so worn as to be shiny, and thus changing from black to blue as the light catches it, is an 'illusion' like the colour of the sky as it changes from night to day–in other words, Cabra's priesthood was a sham. The girdles round religious habits were used as 'disciplines', for doing penance by self-flagellation. Cabra's cassock is worn without a girdle because there is no penance in his priesthood. His description concludes: 'with his long hair and his short cassock, he looked like the lackey of death. Each shoe could have been the tomb of a Philistine.'⁹ A priest should be the guide to salvation, but Cabra is the opposite–the guide to death. He is the opposite because a priest's head ought to be shaven and his garment long, but Cabra's hair is long (*largos*) and his cassock short (*mísera*); but *largo* also means 'generous' and *mísero* 'stingy': Cabra is generous to himself because he encourages his private interests by stinting his priesthood, which should be charity to others. Since he is turned into a guide to death (the death of the spirit), the last parts of him to be described are turned into gigantic tombs so that our final image may be that of the grave swallowing him and all men who are the opposite of what they should be. The wit is brilliant, but it is wit directed to a serious satirical end.

The exposure of human self-conceit is apparent also in a particular type of verbal witticism that is a constant thread running through the style. In describing people or objects connected with them, Quevedo uses an epithet or a phrase that ennobles them, and then, by word-play, shatters the illusion by turning it into its opposite. A simple example is the meal served at the miserly Cabra's boarding-school: the pupils, he says, 'ate an eternal meal'; but since the definition of eternity is that it has no beginning and no end, the food was conspicuous by its virtual absence: *comieron una comida eterna, sin principio ni fin*. This joke must be placed in the context of the clerical schoolmaster who is not a guide to salvation (eternity) but to death. At the end of the novel, the delinquent protagonist is enjoying a social prosperity that is illusory because it contradicts his moral condition; to ape the well-to-do by hanging tapestries on his walls, he buys cast-off armorial hangings from taverns; these, he says, 'were more worth seeing than those the King had'. But the idiom Quevedo uses for 'worth seeing' means literally 'for seeing', so: 'they were more for seeing than those the King had, for you could see through mine because they were so full of holes, while through his you would see nothing.'[10]

This type of joke is applied to every character in the novel except Don Diego Coronel (who is the symbol of reality and goodness contrasted with the illusory world of delinquency). The picaroon's father 'came of a very good stock'–'and considering how he drank one can well believe it'; his brother 'stole everybody's hearts' and was 'a little angel', a term of endearment that would be justified by his being dead, were it not for the fact that he had died in prison because of his powers of attracting objects from other men's pockets. His mother 'had so much charm that she enchanted everybody she dealt with'–'only they said something about a he-goat and flying through the air....'[11] Variants of this type of joke are euphemisms that characters apply to themselves in order to hide the mean reality. The picaroon's father 'was a barber by trade; although his thoughts were so elevated that he was ashamed to be called that, claiming that he was a shearer of cheeks and a tailor of beards.'[12]

So frequent are these jokes, so strong an impression is left on the reader by the phantasmagoria of Quevedo's grotesque world, that most critics have succumbed to the temptation to see nothing more in the plot and the characterization than the occasion for a prolonged display of flashing wit. But just as the grotesque descriptions disclose a serious satirical purpose below the surface of distortion, so, too, are these jokes directed to a similar end. They all show the same technique of pricking a bubble of illusion; since human beings have an infinite capacity for self-conceit, reality can only be reached by exposing their illusions. This is how Quevedo focuses the problem of the delinquent. He writes what is above all a sarcastically funny book, but the psychology of delinquency is seriously conceived and the wit has a structural pattern which harmonizes with the psychological presentation of the protagonist; and not only the wit, for the way the plot itself is constructed contributes to this over-all unity. In common with all other Spanish picaresque novels, *El buscón* has been accused of having no structure but only a jumble of disconnected incidents; C.B. Morris, however, has now demonstrated that it has a structural unity of a subtle and original kind, based on a series of recurring motifs, which, as it were, project the past into the present and the future, 'entrapping' the protagonist, who, seeking to escape from the past, is in effect constantly re-enacting it.[13] The significance of this will be soon apparent.

Quevedo's characteristically laconic Prologue bluntly states the problem of hypocrisy, which, as we have seen, was raised as a crucial issue by Alemán's attitude to his material and by Úbeda's reactions to it. 'Here you will find', says Quevedo to the reader, 'every kind of roguery–which I think most people like–astuteness, deceptions, ingenuities and ways, born of idleness, of living by trickery; and you will be able to derive no little profit from this if you heed the moral lesson–and if you don't derive profit from this then go and listen to sermons, for I doubt whether anyone buys a jocular book to escape from the temptations of his depraved nature.'[14] Readers of novels do not turn to picaresque stories for sermons and

Quevedo is not going to pretend that they do by offering them any. They want the excitement and the fun of picaresque knavery, and that is what he will give them. But this does not mean another ironical work like *La pícara Justina*, or another *Hija de Celestina*, because behind the fireworks of the wit there lies a profound insight into the character of a delinquent. Since this character is revealed as one that gradually empties itself of anything positive until only a void is left, and since the wit itself is so devised that it exposes an empty world behind the social self-assertion of men, the picaresque narrative carries its own moral within it and requires no sermons. The triumph of Quevedo–what helps to make *El buscón* the peak of the picaresque novel–is that the values of morality are intrinsic to the narrative, and that it is impossible to read it correctly without reading it as a profoundly moral story. But to be read correctly, it cannot be read superficially, as it often has been and still is.[15] For it is a novel rich in human truth, one that gives us a psychological study of a delinquent that is far in advance of its time, an analysis of the relationship between character and environment that reaches through the pressure of external circumstances into the heart of the conflict between the individual and society, and probes the inner, deep-seated motives that make a delinquent choose that manner of life rather than another.[16]

Quevedo's picaroon is called Pablos. His father is a thief and his mother a witch. They are notorious figures in Segovia. As a boy, Pablos suffers mercilessly from the taunts of the other boys in the town, who make constant mocking allusions to his parents:

> I put up with everything, until one day a boy dared to
> shout after me that I was the son of a whore and a witch;
> because he said this so clearly–for I would not have
> minded had he said it darkly–I picked up a brick and
> broke his head. I ran to my mother for her to hide
> me... I asked her to tell me whether I could truthfully
> tell the boy he lied, or whether she had conceived me

by giving many men a share, or whether I was the son of my father alone. She laughed and said: 'Gracious me! Do you know about those things already? You're going to be no fool; you've got a sense of humour; you did right in breaking his head, because such things, even though they be true, should never be said.'[17]

The cynicism of this answer is a cruel blow to the boy, leaving him with no defence against the mockery of his companions except flight. 'When I heard this I was as if struck dead; I determined to collect what belongings I could within the next few days and to leave my father's house, so strong was the shame I felt.'[18]

This shame and the accompanying fear of the hostility of society produce in Pablos a deep-seated feeling of inferiority. To cancel the superiority of others he takes refuge in an ideal world of fantasy, in which he eliminates the factor that oppresses him in real life. He lifts himself out of his actual situation as far as his fantasy can possibly take him.[19] Just as his inferiority feeling derives from shame at his parents' social standing and notoriety, so his dreams for the future take a social form, placing him in a social position as far removed as possible from theirs. 'My parents had long arguments about whose profession I was to follow; but I, who had always from childhood had the idea of becoming a gentleman, never applied myself to either.'[20] A pathetic ideal indeed, harmless at this stage, but potentially dangerous.

The first step to becoming a gentleman is to be educated. 'I pacified them, saying that I was firmly determined to learn to live a virtuous life and to persevere in my good resolutions; I therefore asked them to put me to school, because if one couldn't read or write, one wouldn't be able to do anything.'[21] His entry into school brings to the fore another trait in his character which, together with his compensatory fantasy, is to be decisive for his future development. The timid Pablos, requiring the practical compensation of actual praise, goes out of his way to curry favour:

[The master] gave me a cheerful welcome, and told me
I had the look of a sharp-witted and intelligent man.
Because of this, in order not to prove him wrong, I
learned the lessons well that morning. The master used
to make me sit by his side; on most days, as a reward
for being the first to arrive, I was given the cane to
wield; and I was the last to leave because I ran errands
for 'Madam', as we called the master's wife. I was in
their good graces for being so obliging. They showed
me too much favour, and this made the other boys
envious.[22]

This pathetic attempt to compensate for his timidity and
shame only accentuates the unpleasant behaviour of his school-
mates, who make cruel fun of him.

Pablos's first efforts to realize his goal of a gentleman, combined with this toadying, also bring failure. He abandons the
boys of his own class and makes up to those of a higher:

I sought out the sons of gentlemen and people of quality,
and particularly a son of Don Alonso Coronel de
Zúñiga, with whom I shared my lunches. On holidays
I went to his house to play with him, and I kept him
company every day. But the other boys, because I didn't
speak to them, or because they thought I was being too
snobbish, kept on giving me nicknames that recalled
my father's profession.[23]

His failure here is not only social. Since he cannot approach
this young gentleman on terms of equality—because of his
class, but still more because of his timidity and shame—he
makes up to him by a form of flattery, seeking to win his
favour by always denying himself pleasure in order to give it
to his friend:

During all this period I was constantly visited by that
son of Don Alonso Coronel de Zúñiga, who was called
Don Diego; naturally he liked me, because I exchanged
my tops for his if mine were better; I used to give him
part of my lunch, never asking for any of his in return;

> I would buy him picture cards, I taught him to wrestle,
> I played at bull-fighting with him and kept him con-
> stantly amused.[24]

At last Pablos has won for himself affection, and affection from
a person of high social standing, but at the cost of laying the
seed of servility. This flattery is here natural enough, but it is
pointing forward to what Quevedo will later make the decisive factor that plunges him into the career of a delinquent
– the willingness to barter moral independence and self-respect
for the praise of others.

Such conduct leads Pablos into a vicious circle. His efforts
to compensate for the hostility of society serve only to increase
it. One day the two boys see in the street a man called Pontius
Aguirre, who was rumoured to be a Jew. 'Call him Pontius
Pilate and run', says Diego, and Pablos does it 'to please him';
the result is a beating. Another such disaster, which immediately follows, is recounted with a remarkably subtle touch. At
the Shrovetide carnival boys used to tilt at a hanging cock;
one was chosen to be their leader, the 'Cock King', and was
dressed up appropriately. The honour falls to Pablos, to whose
timid and repressed spirit it provides a tremendous satisfaction; with ill-concealed pride he leads the procession 'bowing
to one side and the other like a Pharisee on the march'. His
horse seizes a cabbage as it passes a greengrocer's stall; the
vendor sets up a hue and cry, Pablos is pelted by the market-
women, his horse rears, and he is thrown into a privy. His self-
satisfaction thus ends in a greater humiliation than any that
he had previously suffered; but there is more in the episode
than that:

> And I want to confess to you in passing that when they
> started throwing eggplants and turnips at me, since I
> was wearing feathers in my hat, I thought that they had
> mistaken me for my mother, and that they were throwing
> at her as they had done on other occasions. And so, being
> simple-minded and only a boy, I said: 'Sisters, although
> I am wearing feathers, I am not Aldonza de San Pedro,

my mother', as if they couldn't see that from my clothes
and face. The fear I felt excuses my ignorance, and
the fact that this calamity befell me so suddenly.[25]

Witches were punished by being tarred and feathered, which
is the reason for this strange confusion in Pablos's mind. The
suddenness with which everything happens makes Pablos's
reaction a purely spontaneous one; no defences are interposed,
and fear–fear of the ill-treatment that society is constantly
meting out to him–brings to the fore the dominant element
in his character: his self-identification with his mother's guilt.
This family guilt, he thinks, is what provokes the brutal hostility of society; it results in a humiliation and a shame so
overpowering and so lasting in its effects ('even to recount it
makes me feel afraid', he says), that the memory of it is later
to influence him decisively at a critical moment in his moral
development. For the time being, his only refuge is to escape
from his family and his home town:

> I resolved never to return to school or to my parents'
> house... I wrote home saying that I no longer needed to
> go to school even though I couldn't write well, because
> the first requirement for my intention to become a gentle-
> man was to write badly; and that I was therefore aband-
> oning school to save them expense, and their house to
> save them displeasure.[26]

The hostility of society, in other forms, dogs his steps despite
the change of environment. He follows Don Diego, as his servant, first to Cabra's boarding-school and later to the University of Alcalá; at the former he is all but starved to death; at
the latter, hostility in the form of practical jokes reaches the
extreme of heartless cruelty. In self-defence he is driven to
assert himself, to decide on a course of action that will make
life bearable. Since it is difficult for this timid youth, obsessed
with a fear of society, to stand up to ill-treatment in a resolute
or valiant way, he is more likely to adopt a weak than a heroic
course. There are two weak courses: either he can evade coming to terms with his environment by shrinking into despair,

or he can rise superior to it by excelling it according to its own standards. Pablos finds himself in the society of students; what they seem to admire most is roguery of the practical joker's kind. Among them, he can gain significance only by outrivalling them at their own game, and it is this decision that he comes to. He determines to develop that form of cunning and astuteness that consists in 'getting away with it'.[27] ' "When in Rome do as the Romans do", says the proverb, and it says rightly. After turning it over and over in my mind, I eventually decided to be a rogue among rogues, and more of a rogue than all of them if I could.'[28]

This is the first of two major decisions that are to lead him along the path of delinquency. It is a further, and now a pernicious, example of the weakness that had made him curry favour as a child. Then his success had been only partial, now it is complete; for he wins from all sides the praise he has always yearned for. On the one hand his skill in thieving arouses the admiration of Don Diego for what he takes to be the faithfulness and honesty with which their money allowance is made to go so far; on the other hand, it delights and astonishes the rest of the students, whose applause spurs him on to ever more of these meretricious triumphs. But behind this self-assertion there lies a deeper motive than the quest for flattery—that of revenge for the humiliation of his childhood: 'In order not to be tedious I shall refrain from telling how I turned the town square into a forest, for from the boxes of the cloth-shearers and the silversmiths, and from the stalls of the fruiterers—*since I shall never forget the disgrace I suffered when I was the Cock King*—I fed the fire of our house all the year round.'[29] Pablos is thus revenging himself for the hostility of society by declaring war on it. His actions are antisocial, not by accident but of set-purpose; it is not only praise he seeks but vengeance.

Pablos makes the second major decision when Don Diego is forced to dismiss him from his service. With the newly-won self-confidence that would appear to make his social ambitions realizable, he rejects the offer of useful work befitting his station. Don Diego 'was distressed at dismissing me. He said he would find me a situation with another gentleman among his friends. I, laughing, said to him: "Sir, I am now another man with other ideas; I am aiming higher and need a more influential position." '[30] His own master, he will be a servant no longer: society will be made to accept him as a gentleman. Yet this presumptuousness is still a pathetic day-dream in whose smug and pleasant picture of himself he overcomes the hardness of reality: 'I kept on thinking how difficult it would be for me to live a life of honour and virtue, since it was first necessary to hide how little my parents had had, and then to have so much myself that no one would recognize in me what I had been. So much did I approve of these honourable thoughts that I was grateful to myself for them. I said to my-self: "I, who have not had anyone from whom to learn virtue, or any virtuous person to imitate, shall deserve more thanks than one who has inherited virtue from his ancestors." '[31]

In his home town where, unrecognized, he passes himself off as 'a gentleman of rank', he is soon made to suffer agonies of shame from the patronage of his disreputable hangman uncle, whose brawls he is forced to witness: 'When I saw how honourable were the people who were conversing with my uncle, I confess that I blushed, unable to hide my shame… I was on tenterhooks to get the dinner over, collect my money and flee from my uncle.' 'All this abomination and depravity that I was witnessing made me ever more impatient to be among gentlemen and people of quality.' Pocketing his father's legacy, he therefore departs for Madrid, turning his back on his

---

[5.] Quevedo: a portrait attributed to Murillo. (By courtesy of the Musée du Louvre.) The identification of both artist and sitter is uncertain, but apart from the fact that the nose is here more aquiline, the face resembles that of the authentic portrait of Quevedo, attributed to Velázquez, in the Wellington Museum. Quevedo would here be about sixty years old.

family shame: 'what most comforted me was the thought that I was going to the capital—where nobody knew me'. 'I must repudiate my kin', he writes in his farewell letter to his uncle.[32]

But it is precisely his kin—his ancestral stock—that makes his ambition impossible. He cannot consort with the upper classes on terms of equality, for he has neither birth nor wealth. Inevitably, therefore, he enters into association with those aristocrats who, through penury, have sunk to his own level, and who ludicrously strive by every manner of artful and dishonest deception to keep body and soul together while maintaining genteel appearances. Pablos's ambition, therefore, leads him into delinquency, and his special form of self-confidence confirms him in it. In no other sphere can he hold his own and excel. His cleverness brings him to the verge of success—he gets himself accepted as an equal by 'people of quality' and is about to marry an heiress—but the extravagance of his ambition is his undoing.

There is cruel, if poetic, justice in the manner in which his imposture is unmasked, for this is brought about by the very person to whom, as a boy, he first humbly turned in his efforts to rise above his family shame. It is Don Diego who exposes him—Don Diego who, before establishing his identity, recalls his social stigma when apologizing to the impostor for having thought him to be Pablos: 'You will not believe it: his mother was a witch, his father a thief, his uncle a hangman.' After exposure, Pablos meets his punishment at the hands of the gentlemen with whom he had tried so hard to consort. His arrogant but all too understandable endeavour to 'repudiate his kin' recoils upon him. Attempting to compensate himself for his sense of guilty inferiority, he had pitched his aims inordinately high and is, as a result, plunged into the depths of social disgrace. Because of a moral weakness that had begun as the fruit of ingrained fear and that had grown through

[6.] Pablos as 'Cock King' (see p. 65). From *Obras de Francisco de Quevedo* (Verdussen, Antwerp 1699).

indulgence in self-conceit into the pride of unscrupulous over-confidence, he attempts to impose himself upon a hostile society by cunning and fraud, and becomes a socially un-adapted person, a moral reprobate. At the end he is one of a gang who, in a drunken brawl, murder two policemen. Hunted by the law, he can only go out at night disguised. Tiring of this harassing existence, he emigrates to the Indies with the whore who had shared his home, only to find, as he tells us in his closing sentence, that he fared even worse across the sea.[33] By letting the novel peter out in the hint of continuous decline Quevedo is going to disturb his French translator, but he is in fact giving it an ending that is perfectly fitted to his theme, for by pricking the bubble of the delinquent's inflated ambition, he makes him gradually, as it were, shrivel away into nothingness.

This analysis has been concerned only with the character of the protagonist, but there is still more to *El buscón* than that. No one has written more profoundly on its wider significance than T. E. May, and one of the points he adds to its interpretation should not be overlooked here.[34] Pablos is presented by Quevedo as bearing a burden of guilt and shame that seems to have been imposed upon him from without. The reality and meaning of a guilt of this kind, and its concomitant suffering, could not, says May, be imaginatively sought by Quevedo except in a context of religious belief. The crisis in Pablos's life is the persecution to which, as a freshman, he is subjected on arrival at the university. This brings him to the momentous choice whether he is to seek adjustment to society by accepting his suffering, or reject his suffering and so turn against the society that inflicts it. The form in which Quevedo presents this crucial experience and decision is seen by May as a kind of internally experienced allegory.

As the freshman Pablos makes his way to the lecture rooms on his first morning, the students gather round him, hold their fingers to their noses and say: 'This Lazarus is ready to be raised from the dead, he stinks so much.' They then follow up this mockery of Christ by spitting on Pablos. Christ, mockery and spitting symbolically recall the Passion: Pablos is thus thrust into a situation which parallels that of the suffering Christ. That the Crucifixion is reproduced as a possibility in his mind is revealed by the fact that when, after this torment, he returns to his lodging and to his landlord who looks with astonishment at his shocking appearance, Pablos says: 'I am not *Ecce Homo*.' 'Behold the Man' were the words spoken by Pilate as he brought out the scourged Christ to be shown to the people; and 'Ecce Homo' is the name traditionally given to pictures of Christ at that stage of the Passion. Pablos thus re-calls the Crucifixion, but only to repudiate any connexion between himself and the suffering Christ. He then enters his room, goes to bed, and falls asleep. Since there is no reason why he should sleep in the middle of the morning, May sees this as symbolical of the entombment of Christ that precedes the Resurrection; and, in fact, his master, returning from lec-tures and astonished to find Pablos asleep in bed, wakes him with the words: 'This is now another life.' (Later, after Pablos has decided to seek revenge on society by becoming a delin-quent, he says to his master: 'I am now another man.') This crisis in Pablos's life consequently takes a form which links his sufferings with those of Christ. Thus, according to May, Quevedo sees the supernatural as not only present in the de-linquent's world but as actually thrust upon him. The grief of Pablos is the grief of humanity and this grief is apprehended in a Christian way. The words 'I am not *Ecce Homo*' preface the choice of delinquency and represent the rejection of Christ–Pablos's refusal to take up his cross. The new life to which he awakes is, in accordance with the mockery of the students, a travesty of spiritual resurrection: it is the life of the sinner, not of the saved.

This interpretation is so subtle that one accepts it only after an initial resistance, since the pointers to this symbolism seem too few and too undeveloped to carry so deep a seriousness. Such seriousness, also, might seem incompatible with the wit that describes the episode and the crudity with which the students enact it. But wit (especially in the seventeenth century) is not synonymous with irreverence; everything human, even jesting and depravity, has a bearing on the ultimate seriousness of life; further, this symbolism need not have been present to Quevedo's conscious mind at all–his imagination, the servant of an acute intelligence, could have seized on these images of the Passion for their inner appropriateness while the conscious mind saw their potential wit. It is not necessary to accept this symbolism in order to accept the character study of a delinquent, since the two are independent; but if it is accepted, then *El buscón* is linked, like *Guzmán de Alfarache*, to the religious conscience of the age (which is not to say that it is a religious work); that it is linked to it without any sermonizing, but only by the strength of Quevedo's imaginative vision, is a measure of the greater brilliance of his novel. The brilliance lies also in the way its satirical wit is harmonized with the theme, and above all in its insight into the psychology of a delinquent. The protagonist moves through a stylized world of caricature, but his character is human. Despite what has nearly always been repeated since Chandler, the individual character is here, as in *Guzmán de Alfarache*, more important than the society through which he moves. The character drawing in *El buscón*, though always concise, is consistent and complete. Because Pablos is a rounded character he can arouse our understanding and compassion, all the more so because of the unflinching hardness of the world in which he is placed.

For these reasons, *El buscón* must be considered the masterpiece of the picaresque tradition. It is the zenith to which *Guzmán* marked the rise. Both these two major Spanish picaresque novels show how misguided are those historians of the novel in France and England who dismiss the Spaniards for the incompatibility of their professed moral aims with the nature of their picaresque material. This shows both an ignorance of the historical causes of the picaresque *genre* in the

Counter-Reformation and a misunderstanding of the first approach to picaresque material. Alemán and Quevedo turned to this kind of material because they were profoundly interested in the causes of sin and crime. For Alemán, the causes of sin are explained by moral theology, but an interest in this theology leads him to an interest in practical psychology. Thus he shows insight into the clash between temptation and conscience, and he gives a moving analysis of the psychological and emotional factors behind the process of conversion. In Quevedo, the psychological insight is much more remarkable and it is autonomous; it explores the influence of environment upon the development of character without the intrusion of moral theology.

Both novels must be classed as significant explorations of the problem of the delinquent, and thus as novels that give the new *genre* of the picaresque both literary validity and human depth. What comes after *El buscón* marks only a decline in one or other of the two directions mapped out by *Marcos de Obregón* and *La hija de Celestina*—either that of toning down the harsh colours or that of facetiousness. The middle-of-the-road good-mannered treatment of picaresque material is continued by Alonso de Castillo Solórzano (1584–1648?), a fairly prolific novelist who is a contemporary of Quevedo's, but who is quite lacking in the latter's intelligence and passion. He attempts to make of the picaresque novel an artistic literary form. We find unity of plot and a style with pretentions to elegance. There is no didactic moralizing, no acid wit; neither is there any crude farce or facetiousness; instead, the *genre* assumes an air of refinement in order to amuse polite upper-class readers without shocking them or touching their consciences on the raw. Castillo Solórzano does achieve a consistent level of artistry, but only one of polished mediocrity.[35] The world of criminal life thus becomes something to be treated with well-bred gentility.

The actual nadir of the *genre* in Spain is reached, appropriately enough, by the last work to exemplify the basic elements of the tradition, *Estebanillo González* (1646).[36] Although the end is now reached, forty-seven years after the beginning, and although the French realistic novel has come into existence, an independent picaresque novel, properly speaking, has not yet been born abroad. This last Spanish example is, however, a bridge that leads out of Spain into Europe, into a wider sphere of human delinquency – that of international warfare.

4

Germany and the Thirty-Years War

PAIN'S implication in the Thirty-Years War, bringing with it the continuance of war with France and with her rebellious Dutch subjects, and coming as it did after a century of almost continuous fighting, ruined her economically and led to the eventual loss of her position as a great power. The mounting tide of disaster and crisis brought with it a disenchantment and a sense of depression that are evident in much of Spanish literature, notably in Quevedo. Weariness with war is a note that is strongly struck in 1640 in the *Idea de un príncipe político cristiano* (*Idea of a Christian Political Prince*) by Diego de Saavedra Fajardo. Whereas throughout the preceding century war had been looked upon as natural and heroic, and ardent bellicosity could find its way into print, by Saavedra Fajardo's time it had become possible to preach something near to pacifism. He realizes that war is not only a folly but also a destructive evil, one that saps the strength of nations, and he inveighs against the 'bellicose madness' of Europe and attacks the 'martial ministers' of the nations – the 'warmongers' – who see war as a means of furthering their own glory and self-interest and so look for every possible pretext of waging it.

Estebanillo González (1646) belongs to this period and is the one Spanish prose work that unfolds its story, from beginning to end, in the setting of historical and not imaginary warfare; yet nothing of this pacifist spirit is evident in it. A tale of war in the 'low style', it makes its theme an occasion for jesting rather than for horror. The title is the name of the protagonist and also purports to be the name of the author, for the work claims to be a genuine autobiography. This has been substantiated: the chronology and geography are correct, the majority of the people named are historical and are accurately described.[1] The only thing that cannot be confirmed is Estéban González himself, but since he was only a jester it is not surprising that history does not record his name outside the pages of his book.

The period of the autobiography is the Thirty-Years War, the terrible and senseless calamity that was still devastating Germany when the book was published. This is the background to the career of Estebanillo González. Beginning with a typical picaroon's career in Italy, he becomes a campfollower in the Spanish armies in Germany and Flanders, seizing the opportunities for thieving delinquency that this offers. Finally he becomes the jester of the Imperial commander, Ottavio Piccolomini, Duke of Amalfi; and later, for a time, he becomes the jester of the Governor of the Low Countries, the Prince-Cardinal Don Fernando, brother of Philip IV of Spain. Connected as he thus was with persons of the highest importance, Estebanillo travels over Italy, Spain, France, Belgium, Holland, Germany, Austria, Poland, and even into Russia, and pays one brief visit to England. Apart from the interest of this historical background, the only significance the work has is the significance of decadent literature. It is true that at times it is genuinely funny, notably in the farcical description of the author's attempt to avoid having to take part in the Battle of Nördlingen; but on the whole it is a work that leaves a very unpleasant taste in the mouth. There is a constant wallowing in facetious jokes about drink and drunkenness. What is particularly unpleasant is the completely cynical attitude to life, and the ability to jest crudely about even the most serious and tragic events. In this the book is doubtless realistic, since this cynicism must have coloured the attitude of the common soldier to his profession. One cannot therefore deny it value as a social document, and the fact that it is deficient in seriousness is itself part of this documentary value.

In all the terrible devastation of the Thirty-Years War, never once does Estebanillo show the slightest realization of its horror and its suffering. He is completely devoid of any human feeling, of any sense of compassion, jesting about his drunkenness while men are slaughtered and cities burn around him. It is a completely heartless book; there is nothing, not even his own soul, that he can take seriously. When he kills a soldier in a quarrel and is sentenced to death, he writes: 'The jailor told me to make my peace with God, without in that final extremity giving me the means of making my peace with Bacchus.' This is how he describes his confession before what he thought was to be his execution: 'I cleared the room and getting down on one knee like a crossbowman about to fire, I disgorged all my guilt from its quiver, and I emptied all the shelves in the storeroom of my sins; and after receiving absolution and the blessing, I felt such a new man that my only regret at dying was that I thought, so contrite was I, that all the bells would ring of their own accord, that all Barcelona would be in a commotion, and that all the poor people would lose their wages by coming to see me.'[2] Coupled with this cynical facetiousness, there is something even more unpleasant: his deliberate parasitism on the great, and his eagerness to degrade himself by getting blind drunk, purely to profit financially from the amusement this causes others, are true picaresque qualities in their utter shamelessness.

In *Estebanillo González* we thus have the delinquency of the picaroon related with gusto by someone who delights in being a real-life example of it. The cynical and frivolous insensitiveness to anything that is dignified and decent, the total absence of an atom of self-respect in this last Spanish picaresque work is the justification for the earnestness with which the *genre* began, for it is precisely this degradation of human nature that Alemán felt so intensely and strove with such seriousness to redeem. Less than fifty years, therefore, witness the rise and the fall of the picaresque novel in Spain. *Guzmán de Alfarache* (1599) and *Estebanillo González* (1646) are not only the first and the last, they are also the two extremes–the one, man's anguished awareness of his need for redemption; the other, man's frivolous insensitiveness to his own degradation.

¶ By a satisfying coincidence, the first important non-Spanish picaresque novel has exactly the same setting as the last of the Spanish ones–the Thirty-Years War. This is *Der abenteuerliche Simplicissimus* (*The Adventurous Simplicissimus*) by Hans Jacob Christoffel von Grimmelshausen (1621?–76).[3] It was probably published in 1668, although the first edition is dated 1669. The five Books in which it first appeared present a complete and rounded narrative, but so popular did it prove that Grimmelshausen published a *Continuatio* in 1669, which was added to later editions of the novel as a Sixth Book. Three further *Continuationes* were quickly written, but these have little merit and are generally disregarded. Nothing is added to the theme of delinquency by the Sixth Book or the other sequels.

Apart from the historical setting, there are two links between *Simplicissimus* and *Estebanillo González* in that the protagonist of the former is, for a time, also the jester of army commanders, and that in the course of his wanderings he, too, visits Russia. It has, in fact, been asserted that Grimmelshausen must have known the Spanish work,[4] but the fact that both protagonists are jesters is an understandable coincidence in war novels that had to have a humorous element; it seems clear that there is no influence of the Spanish work upon the German.

Outside Germany *Simplicissimus* is unjustly neglected. Its

omission from general studies of the picaresque novel is one of the factors that have contributed to the diminution of the historical significance of *Guzmán de Alfarache*, for it is this novel and not the earlier *Lazarillo* or the later works of Espinel and Castillo Solórzano that created the picaresque *genre* in Germany. Those scholars who, like van Praag, del Monte and Sobejano, deny the close connexion between *Guzmán de Alfarache* and the Counter-Reformation, do not realize how they give their case away by ignoring *Simplicissimus* and its sources in the Counter-Reformation culture of South Germany. The First Part of *Guzmán* was freely translated into German by Aegidius Albertinus (1560–1620) and published in Munich in 1615, where he was secretary and librarian at the Court. Although Alemán's Second Part had been published eleven years before this, Albertinus was unaware of its existence; he did, however, know Martí's apocryphal Second Part of 1602,[5] which he utilized to complete his First Part; he then added a Second Part of his own.[6] Ignorant of the fact that Alemán had brought his delinquent to repentance and conversion, Albertinus of his own accord makes him undergo a religious conversion and accept a hermit's advice to undertake a pilgrimage to the Holy Land in order to atone for his sinful life. Albertinus's Second Part has scant literary merit, but it does demonstrate that it was natural in Counter-Reformation Europe to see the religious spirit and the religious direction that Alemán had given to his First Part. Albertinus promised a Third Part but never wrote it; instead someone else, disguised under the pseudonym of Martinus Freudenhold, published a Third Part in 1626, in which Guzmán carries out his pilgrimage and then becomes a hermit.[7] This work by Freudenhold has even less literary merit than Albertinus's continuation, but it is historically interesting.

Students of Spanish literature often wonder what form Alemán's promised Third Part would have taken, if indeed they concede that he really intended to write one, for some critics hold that the so-called conversion of his picaroon is so alien to everything that had gone before that it could never have served as the foundation for an organic continuation.[8] In Germany, however, Guzmán is turned first into a pilgrim and then into a hermit. In Spain there was the unpublished Third Part (*c*. 1650) by Machado de Silva, Marquis of Montebelo (1595–1662), to which reference has already been made in another connexion; in this undistinguished and boring work, Guzmán, on his release from the galleys, sets out on a pilgrimage to Santiago de Compostela, takes the habit of the Third Order of St Francis and is, at the end, recommended by the Franciscans to live in a hermitage near a hospital, where each morning he tends the sick.[9] Later, Grimmelshausen has the same pattern. The *Guzmán* of Albertinus and Freudenhold is Grimmelshausen's direct source; he follows up the conversion of his Simplicissimus by making him a hermit, interposing in the *Continuatio* or Sixth Book a pilgrimage to the Holy Land between two phases of his hermit's existence. There is no need to wonder whether there might possibly have been any direct literary contact between Machado de Silva, on the one hand, and Albertinus, Freudenhold, and Grimmelshausen on the other, because there is a long tradition behind all of them. Throughout the Middle Ages the natural thing for a notorious sinner to do after repentance was to atone for his sins by a pilgrimage. For all these continuators of Alemán there was the further point that a pilgrimage fitted into the peripatetic framework of the picaresque narrative. Alemán, if he had written his Third Part, would without any shadow of doubt have made Guzmán a pilgrim and, after that, a hermit. The line of succession from *Guzmán de Alfarache* to *Simplicissimus* is thus unbroken, and this expansion of Guzmán's delinquent career is the only logical conclusion to Alemán's own manner of presenting it. It is necessary to emphasize this because it makes all the more significant the contemporary French rejection of the religious orientation and climax of Alemán's work, which will be discussed in the next chapter.

Simplicissimus is not a novel that can compare in psychological depth, sharpness of wit or brilliance of style with *El buscón*; neither has it got the tautness of feeling that characterizes *Guzmán de Alfarache*—the stretched tightrope along which the delinquent, against the pull of conscience, sways towards social ruin; but none-the-less, *Simplicissimus* has a great deal that they do not possess; it is a masterpiece and a fully original picaresque novel in its own right. Its form is more loose, seemingly more haphazard than that of any Spanish picaresque novel; its narrative is much more crowded, unnecessarily and often bewilderingly so; yet it has been shown to possess a clear symmetrical plan of construction, the original five Books corresponding, in the rise and fall of the novelistic action, to the five-act division of a classical play. Further, there are three symmetrically placed allegorical episodes in the three main sections of the five-act structure, in Book I (exposition), Book III (climax), Book V (dénouement).[10] The first of these (Book I, cap. XV) can serve as an illustration of the special quality of the novel. The boy Simplicissimus, having witnessed a party of peasants savagely tortured by soldiers, ponders on the enmity between the marauding soldiery and the peasantry defending their lives and property.

With such thoughts I fell asleep ill-humouredly, cold and with a hungry belly. I imagined, as in a dream, that all the trees around my dwelling suddenly changed their shape and appearance. On each tree-top sat a cavalier, and the branches were decked with all sorts of fellows instead of leaves; some of these fellows had long spears, others muskets, short guns, halberds, pennants, even drums and pipes. This was a gay picture as everything branched off in a regular and orderly pattern. The root, however, was formed of people of poor esteem, artisans, labourers, peasants and the like, who nevertheless gave their strength to the tree and replaced the fallen leaves out of their own ranks at their own peril. Thereby they complained of those who were sitting on the tree and

this with justification, for the whole weight of the tree
[lay] upon them and pressed them so much that their
money rolled out of their purses and even out of the
seven-times locked treasure chests. If the flow of money
stopped, the commissioners treated them roughly with
brooms (called by one 'punitive expeditions'), so that
sighs escaped from the heart, tears from their eyes,
blood from under their nails, and the marrow from their
bones.[11]

No Spanish picaresque novel shows a similar compassionate
awareness of the suffering and exploitation of the lower classes,
but none, except *Estebanillo González*, has the suffering of war
as its background. Thus, although we move away, as we do
also with *El buscón*, from the strict realism that had characterized the *genre* at the beginning, the tendency to exaggeration,
far from depriving the novel of contact with reality, enhances
its grimness. The horror of war is omnipresent from the very
earliest chapters, and the tone is as different from that of
Estebanillo González as it could possibly be. Often the terrible
senselessness of it all is expressed in bald paradoxes, as in this
description of a battle: 'There could be seen lifeless bodies
despoiled of their own blood and the living covered with the
blood of others.'[12] And the senselessness of it all becomes even
more acute when innocent nature is brought into the chaotic
paradox that man creates: 'Some [of the horses] were seen
falling down dead under their masters, covered with wounds
which they had innocently received in payment for loyal
service. Others fell for the same cause upon the riders, and
gained thus in their death the honour to be carried by those
whom they had had to carry during life. Still others, having
lost their stout-hearted burden which had dominated them,
abandoned humans in their fury and rage, and ran away seeking their first freedom in the open fields.'[13]

The freedom of the open fields which the horses seek, in
their fury to escape from men, is the scene in which both the
beginning and the end of the novel are set. There is an analogy

here with the call of freedom which is one of the keynotes of the Spanish picaresque. In *Simplicissimus* this is in contrast to the battlefield of civilization, and—paradoxically—the freedom of the open field is the life of a hermit. Born, as he thinks, a peasant's son, Simplicissimus as a child sees his cottage looted and destroyed and his family savagely tortured by the soldiers. Fleeing in terror he comes to a hermit who gives him shelter, home, affection, and instruction. At the end, to escape from the captivity of sinful living, Simplicissimus returns to the hermit's life in the freedom of nature. This return at the end back to the beginning is symbolical; part of this symbolism is the very un-picaresque fact of the parentage of Simplicissimus which, of itself, might appear a piece of gratuitous romanticism. At the end he discovers he was not after all the son of a peasant but actually the son of the hermit who had befriended and adopted him as a child, so that the return to the hermit's life in the same forest is the return of the prodigal son to his father's home. Simplicissimus was born of God and must return to God.

This concept of the circle of existence is new to the picaresque novel but it is a familiar one in mystical writings. *La conversión de la Magdalena*, by Malón de Chaide, previously instanced as an example of the only sort of cultural precedent that can be found for *Guzmán de Alfarache*, expounds most beautifully in its opening chapters the circle of love, whereby man, leaving the hands of his Creator, is impelled onwards by love—love of nature, then love of men, then love of ideas, then love of the spirit, to love of God—and so completes the circle of his existence, as Malón de Chaide's heroine, the repentant prostitute Mary Magdalen, completes her circle when she turns from love of man to reach the love of Christ. The affinity of Grimmelshausen with the Spanish religious writers is clear; the close connexion of the picaresque with the Counter-Reformation through *Guzmán de Alfarache* and *Simplicissimus* is indisputable.[14]

But what makes *Simplicissimus* a picaresque novel is, of

course, the hero's career of delinquency. This, like his birth and parentage, shows an original feature, for when as a boy he comes into contact with men after the hermit's death, he is the naivest of simpletons. This gives rise to amusing situations, but it has a serious meaning: he is Simplicissimus and not Stultissimus, because as a child–straight from being fashioned, as it were, by the hands of God–he represents innocence.[15] He cannot understand the ways of the world; everything that men do and aspire to seems to him monstrous folly. So incapable is he of seeing any sense in human life that he is an easy prey for practical jokers; he is taken on a journey to 'hell', then to 'heaven'; he is made to dress as a calf and to pretend that he has been transformed into one. His forbearance is taken for stupidity, and this turns him into a jester of various army commanders. This is the beginning of his corruption, the first movement of the circle away from the love of God towards the love of the world. As mockery begins to sharpen his dormant wits, he realizes that he can only hold his own by playing the role of a witless fool, which is the role of the world. This makes him develop a power of repartee that enables him, like Cervantes's Licentiate of Glass, to tell men some home truths; yet the continued pretence that he has lost his wits means that he is biding his time by the compromise of his integrity. Eventually he is kidnapped by Croat soldiers and later captured by highwaymen. When he escapes he seeks refuge in the forest, where he lives wild. But this return to the forest, thanks to his experience of the world of men, is a travesty of the hermit's life, since prayer gives way to thieving. The convention of the 'many masters', which is a feature of several Spanish picaresque novels, is transformed into the hazards of war. Regiments march along the roads, marauding

---

[7.] Simplicissimus and his hermit father (see p. 83). From the 4th edition, 1671. The caption states that the fool seeks consolation in vanity while the wise man seeks the joy of heaven in God. Each illustration bears the maxim 'Folly deceives'.

Der wahn
betreugt

Der Thor sucht Trost in Eitelkeit
Der Klug in Gott die Himlischfreud.

Der Wahn betreiben

Dem! so man? Unglück offt Pflegt zu? zuschreiben
stösset die Hülffe? Pflantes zu vertreiben.

soldiers roam the countryside, and every time that Simplicissimus is captured he becomes part of the booty and, as a prisoner of war, being too young to serve as a soldier, he becomes a servant to his captor. When he graduates out of boyhood and servanthood, he becomes a marauding huntsman, undertaking forays in which he robs and plunders in order, like Guzmán and Pablos before him, to seek notoriety and fame. The simpleton has become the delinquent.

In Book III all his intelligence is directed to furthering robbery; he makes shoes, for instance, with the heels in front and the toes behind in order to mislead pursuers who follow his tracks. When he gains plunder by turning from thieving to highway robbery, he has at last become 'a proper soldier'. War is thus the delinquency of humanity which produces delinquency in the individual. Every army had its camp-followers in the form of plundering gangs, who were the *Merodebrüder* –the Marauding Brotherhood:

> When a rider loses his horse, or a musketeer his health
> or has to stay behind because his wife and child have
> fallen ill, he easily falls into the company of such rabble,
> a rabble best compared with the gypsies because they
> straggle wantonly in front, behind, around and in the
> midst of the army. And like the gypsies they keep their
> own manners and morals. You can see them in flocks
> like partridges behind the hedges, in the shade or in the
> sun, lingering round a fire, smoking tobacco and idling,
> whilst the honest soldier endures heat and thirst, hunger
> and frost and other miseries with his colours. There a
> pack of them may be looting along in the line of march
> whilst many a poor soldier is near collapse through exhaustion under the weight of his arms. They ravage
> everything they can find before, beside and behind the

[8.] The Dutch ship puts in at Simplicissimus's island (see p. 90). Ibid. The caption affirms that what one generally shuns as misfortune is more often a help.

army; and what they cannot use they destroy so that the
regiments, when they reach their quarters or camp,
often can scarcely find a drink of water. When they are
forced to join the baggage train, one often finds that
this becomes longer than the army itself.... How many
a village have they burned down by carelessness or
malice, how many comrades from their own army have
they robbed of their horses, plundered and even mur-
dered. And many spies may be hidden among them,
knowing the name of a regiment or a company in the
army.[16]

War thus replaces the Original Sin of *Guzmán de Alfarache* as
the background for delinquent behaviour. The bellicosity of
mankind is, of course, a particular instance of Original Sin,
and *Simplicissimus* gains over *Guzmán* by having this immediate, all-pervading particularity. By means of this looting,
and favoured by luck, its hero becomes a rich man and marries.

In Book IV Simplicissimus is a man of the world. His good
looks attract women, and in Paris he becomes the paid lover
of high-born ladies who demand his services. This worldliness
comes to an end when, returning to Germany, he finds he
has contracted smallpox. He loses his good looks; he also loses
all his money. He then becomes progressively a quack doctor,
a 'marauding brother', and the accomplice of a bandit who
ruthlessly murders his victims. When this bandit is killed,
Simplicissimus escapes with his money. He meets Heartbrother, a lost friend, who is so horror-struck that Simplicissimus should be using the bandit's money that he proposes they
undertake a penitential pilgrimage to Einsiedeln. Simplicissimus consents in order to please his friend, and makes a hypocritical pretence at penance. At the Swiss monastery, Simplicissimus sees a devil exorcized, who mocks him for his hypocrisy and accuses him of leading an evil life. This so terrifies
Simplicissimus that he is converted to Catholicism and makes
a general confession. This would, of course, be a *deus ex
machina* if it were the final repentance of the delinquent. But

he has a long way yet to go; since the motive, fear, was an inadequate one for conversion it has no real effect, and before long Simplicissimus has returned to a worldly, dissolute life.

What, then, is the purpose of this episode? It is at least the external adherence to religion and therefore a step in the right direction. That it is a preparation for something better is indicated by two things. First, Simplicissimus has undertaken the pilgrimage for Heartbrother's sake, and he is the only person, apart from his hermit father, whom he has ever loved; it is the only action he has so far done out of love, even though only love of a sort, and the external conversion is a sign of the minimum of ennoblement that this represents. Secondly, the monastery is in a land that is at peace, and peace can have a good influence—even though again, to begin with, only a minimum—on the delinquent fashioned in war:

> The country appeared to me, compared with other
> German lands, as strange as if I had come to Brazil or
> China. I saw the people work and go in peace, the stalls
> were full of cattle, the farmyards filled with fowls,
> geese and ducks, the roads alive with peaceful travellers
> and the inns crowded with people making merry. There
> was no fear of an enemy, no fright of plundering, no
> horror of losing goods, life or limb. Everyone lived safely
> under his own vine and fig-tree and, compared with
> German lands, in sheer happiness and joy, I considered
> this country an earthly paradise although it seemed to
> be rugged by nature.[17]

Simplicissimus marries again and buys a farm. But marriage brings no stability, and both he and his wife are unfaithful to each other. Eventually she dies. Simplicissimus entrusts the management of his farm to his foster-father (whom he has met again and from whom he has learnt his parentage), and retires into the countryside for solitary contemplation. The prelude to his final conversion is the decision he then makes to become a philosopher:

I resolved to aim neither for honour nor gold, nor for
any other thing that the world commonly loves, and I
intended to philosophize and to devote my life to god-
liness, to lament my impenitence, and to strive like my
sainted father to reach the highest degree of virtue.[18]

The allegorical episode of the Mummelsee that follows is a
symbol of this 'philosophizing'.[19] The race of beings who in-
habit the centre of the earth live in a humanist paradise. They
enjoy health and sound reason, with complete freedom from
crime and therefore from punishment. They are, however,
debarred from eternal life and for this reason, in discussion
with Simplicissimus, they refuse to admit that their lot is
better than that of men, and they cannot understand the latter's apparent eagerness to deprive themselves of salvation.
Simplicissimus ironically pretends that the condition of human
society on earth is more consonant with man's spiritual destiny
than it in fact is. They, for their part, can give Simplicissimus
'scientific' information. They explain how the earth is constructed and how water is supplied. When the King promises
to grant him any wish, Simplicissimus asks only for a medicinal
spring to rise on his farm. He intends that this should heal
the ills of humanity without doctors, whose incompetence is
expensive for their patients. But while Simplicissimus genuinely hopes to ease the suffering of humanity, his philosophizing has not yet transcended self-interest, for he also hopes to
do good business by building a large spa to attract a numerous
and rich clientele. But because these are proud and selfish
fancies, they come to nothing. Losing his way, he cannot find
his farm, and his spring gushes out in a forest. He offers its
exploitation to the woodmen, holding out to them the prospect
of prosperity:

But instead of being grateful to me they started to
curse and to shout that I should move myself with my
spring to another place, for if the lord of the manor
would hear of it, the whole district of Dornstetten
would have to do forced labour and build roads to the

place, which would bring great burdens upon them.

'On the contrary,' I replied, 'you will all have advantage from it, for you will sell your fowls, eggs, butter and cattle for better money.'

But they said: 'No, no, his lordship will instal an innkeeper who alone will grow rich whilst we will be his fools to keep the roads and bridges in order, thereby getting no thanks!'... 'We would truly be fools to cut a rod for our own behinds: rather may the devil fetch you and your spring. Haven't you heard already enough why we don't like it?'[20]

There are limits to the practical utility of 'philosophy' since the beneficent healing powers of nature are nullified by men's cupidity and injustice.

Warfare returns to put a stop to all philosophizing. Swedish troops are billeted on his farm, the peasants flee from the land and Simplicissimus himself is persuaded to rejoin the army and eventually to go to Russia in hopes of well-paid service with the Czar. He uses his knowledge of the (non-beneficent) powers of nature to manufacture gunpowder for the Russians. Captured by Tartars, he passes, as previously in his boyhood, from master to master until he eventually becomes a galley-slave. Rescued by the Venetians, he makes a pilgrimage to Rome and Loretto and finally returns home.

The Peace of Westphalia has been signed. The war is over. Books become his only work and his only pleasure. He begins, like Guzmán in the galley, to review his whole life. Where has it brought him? What has he gained from so many vicissitudes? Only the change from innocence to godlessness:

After my blessed father's death, when I came into this world, then I was simple and pure, sincere and honest, truthful, humble, meek, temperate, chaste and modest, pious, devout. But soon I became wicked, false, lying, vain, restless and thoroughly godless, and I have learnt all these vices without a master.[21]

Weary in body, troubled in mind, with the best years of his

life gone, there is nothing that gives him any pleasure: he is an enemy to himself. Experience of the world has brought only disenchantment, and he becomes a hermit. He would have liked to go to the forest where his mineral spring is flowing, but the peasants are still fearful of its exploitation and send him away. He therefore returns to the woods where he was born and in which he had lived with his hermit father. This is the original end of the novel, and this closing of the circle—this return to God and Nature in the same spot where he had emerged from God's hands—is the right and fitting end.

The *Continuatio*, or Book VI, takes Simplicissimus on further travels round the world which add nothing to the significance of the work until the last nine chapters are reached; these add impressively to the symbolism of the renunciation of the world. Simplicissimus is shipwrecked, together with a Portuguese carpenter, on an uninhabited island off Madagascar. The perfect climate, the luxuriant tropical vegetation and the abundance of birds and fishes reveal Nature's beneficence, which the carpenter proceeds to abuse by distilling palm-wine; he soon kills himself through intoxication. Simplicissimus is thus once more a hermit, living under the sign of the Cross which he erects on the island, and seeing in the world of Nature the symbols of Christ's atonement for the delinquency of humanity. He makes ink and writes his life-story on large palm leaves by the light of glow-worms. But his peace is shattered when a Dutch ship puts in at the island and he is once more among men. The sailors sack and destroy his hut and track him down to a cavern, but when they try to enter it, their torches are extinguished and those who had plundered his dwelling go mad. Receiving from the Captain the assurance that he will be left in peace, Simplicissimus reveals himself inside the cavern by the light of his glow-worms and cures the sailors' madness. Since he refuses to return with them to Europe, they rebuild his hut and leave him, the Captain taking away his book for Europeans to read.

The symbolism of cavern, glow-worms and the curing of the

insanity of human strife is a beautiful ending to the whole work which more than compensates for any alleged short-comings of characterization. The imaginative vision of this kind of Baroque writing makes it trivial to complain that Grimmelshausen does not portray a 'developing personality'.[22] Although the conversion of Simplicissimus does not flow from any profound theological insight, this does not mar the religious quality of the book, for this does not lie solely in the final act of renunciation of the world: it lies in the whole conception of the novel, in its circular structure away from the home of a father, who is not known to be such, and back to it after experience of life teaches man from whence he has sprung. Above all it lies in the central symbolism, the contrast between the solitude of nature and the society of men, which is the brutality and the plundering of war.

Yet because the theology has been considered inadequate, it has been alleged that the novel has the serious defect of demonstrating the opposite of what it intends. Gutzwiller argues that the growth of disenchantment in Simplicissimus is only a surfeit of life, a disgust at the world, and not repentance and love of God. The return to the hermitage is an act of pride since it is based solely on human wisdom; it is also a miscalculation since it assumes that a proud contempt of the world is also love of God. Simplicissimus achieves salvation not by fear and trembling but by trusting to his own merit: he asks not for grace but for reward. He becomes a bigger fool than ever before because he identifies folly with the hurly-burly of the world and thinks he can be freed from it by renunciation. But not even a hermit sage can overcome the folly inherent in himself, because this is man's Satanic legacy, from which only God's mercy can free him after death. Gutzwiller therefore concludes that Grimmelshausen's position is close to Pelagianism, since he appears to identify religion with morals and assigns only a passive role to God, taking it for granted that salvation can be achieved by obeying the commandments, those of the Church as well as of God, and by performing 'good works' in order to store up merit.[23]

This is, of course, criticism from the standpoint of Calvinist theology, which Grimmelshausen did not wish to exemplify because he did not profess it. In any case, what is relevant to literary criticism is not the question of the objective or absolute truth in the theology an author chooses to exemplify, but whether he succeeds in giving any *human* truth to his exemplification of it. Not only Grimmelshausen but the literature of his age in general, and especially many Spanish writers, including Alemán, are still often criticized for a 'pessimism' that denies human values, that is not, as the phrase goes, 'life-enhancing'. The value of this literature is often minimized by being dismissed as 'dogmatic'. It is rarely realized that this so-called pessimism is not conterminous with its religious formulation, but springs from a universal and deep human experience. Bertrand Russell, who is no Christian, once formulated a 'free man's worship' in these terms:

Freedom comes only to those who no longer ask of life that it shall yield them any of its personal goods that are subject to the mutations of Time.

Although the necessity of renunciation is evidence of the existence of evil, yet Christianity, in preaching it, has shown a wisdom exceeding that of the Promethean philosophy of rebellion. It must be admitted that, of the things we desire, some, though they prove impossible, are yet real goods; others, however, as ardently longed for, do not form part of a fully purified ideal. The belief that what must be renounced is bad, though sometimes false, is far less often false than untamed passion supposes; and the creed of religion by providing a reason for proving that it is never false, has been the means of purifying our hopes by the discovery of many austere truths....

But passive renunciation is not the whole of wisdom; for not by renunciation alone can we build a temple for the worship of our own ideals.... Except for those rare spirits that are born without sin, there is a cavern of darkness to be traversed before that temple can be entered. The gate of the cavern is despair, and its floor is paved with the gravestones of abandoned hopes. There Self must die; there the eagerness, the greed of untamed desire must be slain, for only so can the soul be freed from the empire of Fate. But out of the cavern the Gate of Renunciation leads again to the daylight of wisdom, by whose radiance a new insight, a new joy, a new tenderness, shine forth to gladden the pilgrim's heart.

...From that awful encounter of the soul with the outer world, renunciation, wisdom, and charity are born; and with their birth a new life begins.... To abandon the struggle for private happiness, to expel all eagerness of temporary desire, to burn with passion for eternal things—this is emancipation, and this is the free man's worship.[24]

This freedom through renunciation is a fundamental human experience and, because it is a confrontation of the naked soul with the universe, it is also one that is deeply religious. It is an experience accessible to theist and atheist alike, and therefore, potentially, to every reader of Baroque literature. The difference between theist and atheist comes later in the content and direction given to the 'charity' that renunciation awakens in them. This freedom is the goal to which Alemán and Grimmelshausen, expressing it in the language of their creed and age, lead their delinquents. Bertrand Russell's 'cavern of darkness', whose gate is despair, is the same cavern of Simplicissimus which extinguishes the world's torches and is lit only by the glow-worms, which are Russell's 'daylight of wisdom'. *Guzmán de Alfarache*, had it been completed, must have led unfailingly to an analogous 'cavern'; as it is, by bringing the delinquent to 'the top of that mountain of miseries' from which either hell or heaven can be easily reached, it brings him to the threshold of renunciation, which he crosses on the torture-rack when he 'dies to Self' by being freed from self-pity in pity for all mankind.

The originality of *Simplicissimus* in relation to the Spanish picaresque tradition has been overstressed in the wrong directions through unfamiliarity with the latter. The statement that the Spanish *pícaros* were 'content to scramble for material success alone' and that only Grimmelshausen offered a character 'who was ultimately fundamentally concerned with his moral and spiritual welfare',[25] is just not true. Grimmelshausen's originality has also been asserted in three other respects: first, that he conceived the character of his delinquent on a deeper level than was usual in the picaresque *genre*; secondly, that he related his plot more closely to contemporary history than any Spanish novel had tried to do; and thirdly, that his work is permeated with his own experiences and is a 'personal document' in a way that no Spanish novel is.[26] All these statements need to be modified: Guzmán is conceived on as deep a level and Quevedo's Pablos on a deeper one; *Estebanillo González*, although a greatly inferior work, is connected with contemporary history from beginning to end; both it and *Marcos de Obregón* are much more autobiographical than *Simplicissimus*.

None-the-less, Grimmelshausen's originality is very great. It must not be looked for on these levels but rather in its remarkable expansion of the picaresque pattern, first by rounding off the religious conversion of the delinquent and particularly by exemplifying it within the 'circle of existence'; and secondly by placing, far more successfully than *Estebanillo González*, the delinquency of mankind in the context of the ghastly horror of war. While in execution it is more uneven than *Guzmán de Alfarache*, and in tone often coarser, it is a more varied and more vivid work.

¶ Grimmelshausen's originality within the picaresque tradition is further apparent in a second novel: *Die Landstörtzerin Courasche* (1670),[27] whose heroine is the ancestress of Brecht's *Mother Courage*. The precedent for the female delinquent was *La pícara Justina*, which had been translated into German from the free Italian rendering of 1624 under the title *Die Landstörtzerin Justina Dietzin, Picara genannt* (1627). No connexion between *Courasche* and this translation of Úbeda has been established. Grimmelshausen might not have thought of a female rogue but for the earlier work, and that is as far as the latter's influence probably goes.

Courasche is a typical picaresque novel not only in form but in the fact that the heroine has to fend for herself from an early age in a hostile world. It is particularly hostile in her case because she is a woman in a world of men at war. 'I would have liked to change my ways', she records, 'but neither habit nor the company I kept would let me better my lot. That's how it goes in times of war: most people become worse rather than better.'[28] She, like Simplicissimus, with whom she at one time associates, is a child of the Thirty-Years War. While she is disguised as a boy she can hold her own, and since she grows up among soldiers, she develops fearlessness and physical courage; but when she is unable to conceal her sex any longer, it is impossible for her not to come to terms with war by means of it. She has a series of soldier husbands, but just as the war never ends so her erotic desire grows insatiable, until she becomes, in fact, a regimental whore. She remains always in command of all situations; since her husbands are killed one after the other and since she is barren and has no children, she has only herself to think of. Relentlessly she makes money: by her amorous services, by becoming a sutler, by booty, by looting, cheating, stealing. Whatever she loses she strives to make good again, living up to her nickname Courage by never despairing. None-the-less her career is a steady decline. Her husbands or paramours are progressively of lower status: cavalry captain, infantry captain, lieutenant, sutler, musketeer and finally gypsy. The total loss of her material fortune coincides with the loss of her physical attractions, a loss that is precipitated by syphilis.

A significant element in the design of the plot is that her erotic vitality is conterminous with the war, whoring being the degradation of women as fighting and looting are of men. This activity of hers does not cease until peace comes. After the Imperial victory at Nördlingen, she feels certain that she will be safe for the rest of her life from the enemies of the house of Austria; she therefore invests her capital in a farm with the hope of settling down. But the war does not end: troops march through and demand winter quarters, her house is requisitioned and heavy financial contributions are exacted from her. Inevitably she becomes familiar with all the officers, and her farm is a centre of wining, dining and whoring. Eventually she is arrested and condemned for her loose living, her property is confiscated and she herself banished: 'What could I do? Had they chosen to treat me more sternly, I would have fared worse. But, well, this was in the midst of the war and every man (I should say "every woman") thanked heaven that the town was getting rid of me, no matter how.'[29] She therefore rejoins the troops and, resourceful as ever, starts trading among them in tobacco and brandy. Finally she joins the gypsies attached to the Swedish army:

> A lieutenant of the gypsies observing that I had some money, a real talent, and a clever hand for stealing, and other virtues useful among this kind of people, lost no time in making me his wife. For me, this had at least the advantage that I no longer needed either oil, creams, or tints and powder to make myself up to look white and beautiful, since my social rank as well as my husband required that I be of the very hue which is called the Devil's favourite colour. From smearing goose-drippings and various salves for lice on my skin and from the use of other unguents to dye my hair, I soon looked as hellish as though I had been born in the heart of Egypt. Often I was so struck by the change I had under-gone that I had to laugh at myself out loud.[30]

This cynical blackening of her once beautiful face symbolizes the change in her activity brought on both by advancing age and by peace. The war ends, but, because she is unable to give up stealing, Courage does not abandon the gypsies. From now on she lives a life not of whoring but of delinquency; this is her peace-time existence.

The end of the novel is left apparently open, as in *El buscón*. An aimless roaming accompanied by 'rascally and thievish tricks' represents the same hardening into the picaresque existence as in Quevedo. Courage was thirteen when her story started (the year was 1620), she was therefore forty-one when peace was concluded. At the time of writing she refers to herself as 'an old woman'. The account of how she came to dictate her autobiography is given in a third novel that forms part of Grimmelshausen's 'Simplician Writings': *Der seltsame Springinsfeld* (1670).[31] A student captured by gypsies is compelled by their 'queen' to write down her life-story; she appears as a magnificent woman, bejewelled and splendidly dressed. Her age is given as between sixty and sixty-six. The first chapter of *Courasche* makes it clear that she has now no intention of repenting, despite the fact that death will soon be knocking at her door. She is a hardened sinner who feels no repentance because she cannot renounce avarice and envy. Her story is a travesty of a general confession for its motive is to avenge herself on Simplicissimus by ridiculing him and vaunting her past life.[32] By stressing this impenitence in her old age Grimmelshausen is scarcely leaving her ultimate fate open: he is in effect leaving her at the gates of hell. This is a departure from the Spanish tradition[33]; so is also the conception of a character who is both perversely wicked and yet, in at least one respect, not unworthy of some admiration.

The word *courasche* 'is army slang, a rough equivalent of the English word *guts*, denoting the raw physical courage of the male animal. This soldier's term for a virtue particularly associated with men of action, but here applied to a woman, connotes an earthiness, even a vulgarity, in German which it is impossible to render into English without losing many word-plays and considerably weakening its symbolical force.'[34] This nuance in the name Courage is confirmed by the setting and tone of the novel. Throughout it there is no love, affection, kindness or unselfishness: it is a godless, ruthless and brutal world. But in the midst of the degradation of war human beings can show courage. Although Grimmelshausen presents this as basically the courage of the wild-beast–the will to survive–it yet has a certain majesty about it, represented by Courage's appearance as the gypsy queen, bejewelled and magnificently dressed despite her blackened face. She is thus not only more wicked but also more vital than Justina who preceded her or Moll Flanders who comes after. The great originality of Grimmelshausen is to have presented the ambivalence of this vitality when set against the background of war. Women as well as men are degraded by 'civilization': instead of a mother–the exemplar of altruistic love–we have in *Courasche* the ruthless, self-seeking, regimental whore, who is courageous but barren.

The tradition that Alemán initiated comes to an end in Germany with Grimmelshausen. In the last decades of the seventeenth century the German novel begins to shift its interest from the world of the picaresque to the values of a bourgeois society. The protagonists learn trades in order to earn honest livings; they become apprenticed to merchants; the usefulness and respectability of commercial activity is stressed, as well as the fact that it has divine approval. Dishonesty now is not so much a sin as an activity that undermines the merchant's credit and so leads to bankruptcy. The Age of Enlightenment has arrived.[35]

5

The Picaresque Tradition in England and France

UTSIDE Germany the Spanish picaresque tradition has a creative influence in Western Europe only in France and England. There are early translations into Italian (among others, *Guzmán de Alfarache*, First Part, in 1606; *La pícara Justina* in 1624; *El buscón* in 1634), but the influence of the *genre* in Italy is negligible.[1] The two Dutch translations of *El buscón* (1642 and 1699) are both made from French versions; that of *Guzmán* (second edition 1665) is very much abbreviated. The *genre* itself does not take root in Holland; the novels that derive from it in form, and that begin to appear from 1679, all transform delinquency into a series of amorous adventures.[2]

With the one exception of the Italian *Justina* priority in all the translations belongs to France; but since the picaresque tradition preserved closer contact with delinquency in England than in France, it is convenient to deal with these countries in this order. The world of Defoe is much tougher and coarser than that of Lesage.

Both Parts of *Guzmán de Alfarache* were translated into English by James Mabbe and published in 1622 with the title

The Rogue.[3] This proved very popular. Although Mabbe's translation of *La Celestina* was never reprinted, his *Rogue* saw five editions in eleven years and was still reprinted after that.[4] While Mabbe does not match in English the conciseness of Alemán's style and thus rather lengthens the work, he remains, despite certain freedoms, fundamentally faithful to the tone and to the plot of the original. The first English translation of *El buscón* is 1657; this will be referred to again later. The best known of the works written under the influence of these translations is *The English Rogue described in the Life of Meriton Latroon* which was begun by Richard Head in 1665, continued by Francis Kirkman in 1668, and completed by Kirkman and Head together in 1671. The name Latroon is of course the Spanish *ladrón* (robber), and the Prologue mentions *Guzmán* and *El buscón* as the sources from which some readers may allege that the material has been collected. While the external form is borrowed, the tone is new: vulgar, coarse, and pornographic. The work is not serious literature; it develops the theme of delinquency into a sensationalism that was never reached in Spain. Meriton Latroon is a real criminal, a corrupt and in no way sympathetic character. This sensational literature produced a *Dutch Rogue* and an *Irish Rogue* and led to the popularity of biographies of criminals.[5] Defoe wrote several short biographies of this kind and is said to have interviewed two notorious criminals in prison. He was not averse to exploiting this new sensationalism: the full title he gave *Moll Flanders*, for instance, was clearly intended to attract purchasers (Plate 9).

There is no serious literary descendant of *Guzmán* here; but English literature does show a work that has many affinities with Alemán's *Rogue*. This is *The Life and Death of Mr Badman* (1680) by John Bunyan (1628-88). Chandler first called this a romance of roguery. While finding in it 'no conscious echo of the merry music of Spain', he pointed out that the prefaces of Alemán and Bunyan struck the same chord ('where one sets up a beacon, the other fires a shot of warning to the wicked'), and he maintained that Bunyan 'subscribed to the picaresque scheme in setting up an anti-hero as anti-thesis to the hero of *The Pilgrim's Progress*'.[6] Ernest Baker indignantly dismissed this suggestion and since his day nobody, as far as I know, has placed *Mr Badman* into the context of the picaresque tradition, though critics who have dealt with it insist that it must be considered a realistic novel.[7] 'It is entirely off the mark', said Baker, 'to compare this powerful didactic work with picaresque fiction. It is radically different. The essence of the rogue-story is light-hearted though sour and biting comedy, even if an Alemán interlards the comedy with incongruous sermons.'[8] This typifies the traditional attitude to the Spanish picaresque novel which it is the purpose of these pages to suggest we should abandon. There is no 'light-heartedness' or 'merry music' whatsoever in *Guzmán de Alfarache*, and what difference of tone there is between it and *Mr Badman* does not justify rejecting Chandler's classification of the latter as a picaresque novel.

Both works should be compared on a broader basis. Bunyan's novel has a dualistic structure similar to Alemán's. Wiseman relates Mr Badman's life-story to his friend Attentive and the two intersperse the narrative with comments on sin in general and Mr Badman's vices in particular. Alemán's work stems from the Counter-Reformation's condemnation of secular literature and itself includes an attack of this kind. The English Puritans were, of course, also strongly opposed to all worldly literature, and in Bunyan's novel Mr Badman goes down hill by reading 'beastly romances' instead of the Scriptures. Both books start with an emphasis on Original Sin of which the respective stories are to be illustrations.[9] There are certain similarities in the careers of the two protagonists. Both are married twice; the first time both marry for money; the second time both wives turn out to be dissolute. Both embark on business careers and both go bankrupt. Near the end of one novel Guzmán feigns sanctity in order to exploit the charity of the pious; near the end of the other novel Mr Badman feigns repentance. It is not impossible that Bunyan could have heard of Mabbe's popular translation, even if he never read any of it; and the existence of *The English Rogue* might have led him to write this counterpart to *The Pilgrim's Progress*. The similarities between *Guzmán* and *Mr Badman* do not, however, add up to any direct influence; but there is a relationship between the two works arising from their both being the literary products of movements of religious reform. Although the authors are on different sides of the theological fence, what they write about is mostly the Christian moral teaching they have in common; and both the books are religious treatments of the theme of delinquency. *Mr Badman* should be classed with *Simplicissimus* as a picaresque novel of the type exemplified by *Guzmán de Alfarache*. Its principal departure from this tradition is that it does not save the sinner but, allowing him to die unrepentant, consigns him to hell in order to drive fully home the sterner Puritan lesson. The repentance and conversion of the sinner remain, none-the-less, the main tradition in England: this is a feature of several of the criminal biographies and is retained by Daniel Defoe (1660–1731), who marks the peak of the picaresque tradition in England.

Moll Flanders (1722) is generally considered the best of his novels of delinquency. Older critics took it as axiomatic that this was a picaresque novel, but more recently, beginning with Ernest Baker and continuing down to Robert Alter, there has been the tendency to deny this on the grounds that it is not a comic work but a novel with a 'sociological significance', one in which Defoe offered 'a serious study of the effects of heredity and environment in the making of criminals'. In the light of *El buscón* this is precisely a reason for retaining it within the picaresque tradition. There are, in fact, three elements in the subject-matter that ally it closely with its Spanish predecessors. First, the heroine is the illegitimate daughter of a woman imprisoned for thieving and therefore has the disreputable origins that are the first postulate of the Spanish picaroons. Secondly, despite her origins and her humble upbringing, she is fired as a girl with the desire to be a gentlewoman: this is exactly the same as the aim of Pablos in Quevedo's *Buscón* to become a gentleman. Thirdly, in her attempted rise, Moll eventually sinks into infamy from which she is finally redeemed by a religious conversion: this is the pattern of *Guzmán de Alfarache*. In subject matter there is, therefore, no divergence from the Spanish ancestry, and for this reason *Moll Flanders*, in literary history, must rank as a picaresque novel. This is not to assert that these or any Spanish novels were direct sources. Defoe could have found these elements in the translations of *Guzmán* and *El buscón*, but he could also have found them in the criminal biographies. These latter were, in any case, part of the tradition begun in England by Mabbe's *Rogue*, and all that need be asserted is that *Moll Flanders* derives from this tradition. The links with the Spanish novels are clear enough, even though the connexion may be indirect and remote.

While the aim of presenting the corruption and redemption of a sinner is the same as that of *Guzmán de Alfarache*, there is a very marked difference. Moll is a good woman to begin with. Her first lapse from virtue is perfectly excusable: she is deceived by a man who promises to marry her, and she loves him. This is followed by deceit in accepting his brother as a husband without telling him of the liaison; but this deceit is understandable and not a vicious fault. She then leads a respectable and comfortable life, which is terminated only by the accident of her husband's death, which leaves her alone in the world. She now practises the deception of appearing as a woman of greater fortune than she actually possesses, but this is only a minor fault for she never directly lies about it, and the happiness of the marriage she then contracts is not in the least minimized by her lack of fortune. This second happy marriage is terminated by another accident – the discovery that her husband is in fact her brother. It is only now that she drifts into being the mistress of a married man. Later, thinking she was marrying a rich man, she finds she has married a poor one, who then turns out to be a highwayman. All these ups and downs are merely accidental and not the result of moral choices on her part. Only when she finally faces the threat of destitution does she turn thief, and come to delight in crime to the extent of preferring not to abandon it when she has become sufficiently rich. But this follows on a long period of matrimonial adventures that have revealed no criminal trait in her character, and the sudden change to delinquency is not therefore psychologically motivated; it is effected only by the compulsion of necessity, and this is not particularly plausible since we can assume that even in 1722 it could not have been impossible for a respectable matron to find the means of earning an honest living. She is, therefore, very far from being a tormented character like Guzmán.

As a result of her delinquency, Moll, like Guzmán, lands in disaster and repents in prison. But her conversion is very different from his. She has all her wits about her at her trial and argues her case with an aplomb that shows no dejection or despair, because she is still hopeful that she will live. Only when the sentence of death is passed does she respond to the persuasions of a minister of religion and undergo repentance and spiritual conversion. Instead of, as is the case with Guzmán, having her constancy put to the test by even greater suffering, Moll is reprieved, sentenced not to death but to transportation to Virginia. From that moment there is no further sign of any spiritual transformation; there is only the practical question of getting over the difficulties and attaining a respectable position once again. It is true that she does not return to evil ways; but it is also true that she no longer shows any concern about God. Although she has in her possession a considerable sum of money, all of it stolen, she never thinks of making restitution; instead, this money is utilized to better her fortune and that of her highwayman husband whom she meets again in prison. By means of this stolen money she changes their status from transported criminals to independent and prosperous planters. Then comes the windfall of her mother's legacy. Now that they are rich and permanently secure their thoughts turn to virtue and religion, and since God has favoured them with material rewards they become sincere penitents for their past lives. The thieves have prospered and so turned pious. How different the end of *Guzmán de Alfarache*! There the criminal, tortured and suffering, feels pity for the first time, pity for mankind because of man's inhumanity to man.

Is it fair to point this contrast? Can Defoe mean what he clearly says? Such is the disparity between this ending and the moral intentions he had expressed in the preface, so glaring is this lack of a serious design in the novel and so shallow his moral attitude to his creation, that a minority of critics, finding all this incompatible with Defoe's intelligence, have turned to irony as the only explanation: Defoe is exposing not a shallowness in himself but hypocrisy in his heroine and in the society of which she is a product.[10] Such an interpretation cannot be successfully defended. Ian Watt has convincingly shown that '*Moll Flanders* is undoubtedly an ironic object, but it is not a work of irony'. This is because we are, in our present age, unconsciously inclined to take ironically what Defoe and his age treated seriously:

Among these predispositions, these ironigenic attitudes, two at least are strongly aroused by *Moll Flanders*: the guilt feelings which are now fairly widely attached to economic gain as a motive; and the view that protestations of piety are suspect anyway, especially when combined with a great attention to one's own economic interest. But, as we have seen, Defoe was innocent of either attitude. He was not ashamed to make economic self-interest his major premise about human life; he did not think such a premise conflicted either with social or religious values; and nor did his age. It is likely, therefore, that one group of apparent ironies in *Moll Flanders* can be explained as products of an unresolved and largely unconscious conflict in Defoe's own outlook, a conflict which is typical of the late Puritan disengagement of economic matters from religious and moral sanctions.[11]

Criticism of *Moll Flanders* from the moral and psychological standpoints is a criticism of the age rather than of Defoe's artistry. This is of a quite different kind from that of any picaresque novelist so far considered. It is realism of a new type: we are much less aware of an author behind the narrative and thus in much closer, more intimate contact with the narrator. Life unfolds itself before our eyes more naturally, not forced into any predetermined grooves. It is an art that conveys the sense of life as the characters actually live it; so much so that the verisimilitude gives the impression of being quite artless. Within it Moll can appear as an engaging woman, very much alive, humanly endearing even in the way she repents with perfect sincerity while in practice doing nothing about it. Ultimately, however, this sympathy established between reader and character cannot give the novel an intellectual solidity that can see life whole, not only on the surface, and give it a pattern of depth and significance; in this respect it falls short of its important predecessors in the tradition.[12]

It must be emphasized, however, that Defoe's attitude to delinquency is markedly different from those of Alemán, Quevedo or Grimmelshausen. One is aware both of a different 'philosophy' and a different attitude to the delinquent. Defoe would seem to uphold a 'natural' morality based on 'natural' standards imposed by the law of reason.[13] Moll aims at economic success and achieves it by means of stolen money for which no restitution is made after repentance. The aim is justified as natural and its rightness is therefore taken for granted; the method is condoned since she steals in the first place out of necessity. Such a purely pragmatic attitude to delinquency is deducible from Defoe's unqualified and un-ironical sympathy for his delinquent. Because of this sympathy *Moll Flanders* has been considered a watershed in the literature of delinquency:

Before January 27, 1722, there was perhaps no con-

siderable literary work in the world which was based
on an intelligent and sympathetic understanding of the
misfortunes of an unprotected woman in contemporary
society...the common attitude of writers before Defoe
was a scornful presentation of the criminal or the fallen,
or a jesting presentation of sullied humanity as a subject
for mirth.

To Defoe, always seeing human experience with the
eyes of a social historian, vice and crime were subjects
not for scorn or mirth but for sympathetic concern.[14]

We must acquire a sense of historical proportion and critical
balance. To say that Alemán, Quevedo and Grimmelshausen
present their criminals scornfully or jestingly is at best a half-
truth; to put it forward as the whole truth is to debase into a
crude simplicity what is in fact a complex attempt to strike a
just, and necessarily painful, balance between divine law and
human reality. For Defoe there is no problem, and no pain in
according sympathy; the simplification and crudity are all on
his side. *Moll Flanders* can indeed be considered a watershed
in the literature of delinquency, but the division lies between
the complex, ultimately pessimistic, response of the seventeenth century to the human condition, and the simple, ultimately optimistic, response of the eighteenth. It must readily
be granted that Defoe's attitude is much more humanitarian
than that of his predecessors, and that there is in him a sociological interest that is foreshadowing an economically and
socially less cruel world. If it were a question of choosing one
of these four writers as a social worker one would unhesitat-
ingly choose Defoe; but imaginative literature is not sociology.

Defoe's humanitarian sentiments are still more apparent in
the novel that followed *Moll Flanders* in the same year of publication, *The History and Remarkable Life of the truly Honourable Colonel Jacque commonly called Colonel Jack*. This shows
the same two features of the picaresque tradition as are in the
earlier work: the protagonist is imbued from an early age with
the desire to become a gentleman, and he undergoes at the end

a religious conversion. It is a much less interesting novel than *Moll Flanders*, being full of tedious and unnecessary adventures that deprive it of any real unity. In his preface Defoe stresses his religious aim:

> Every wicked reader will here be encouraged to a change, and it will appear that the best and only good of an impious, mis-spent life is repentance: that in this there is comfort, peace and oftentimes hope, and that the penitent shall be returned like the prodigal, and his latter end be better than his beginning.[15]

Defoe is once again concerned to show the practical advantages of conversion: Jack, like Moll, prospers materially.

He is the illegitimate son of parents of quality, left by his father in charge of a foster-mother who is told to instil into the boy the belief that he is a gentleman so that he may act like one. Before Jack is ten his foster-mother dies and he and other boys are thrown on their own resources. Homeless in London, they become pickpockets and are later taught to take part in highway robberies; but all the time Jack has an instinctive abhorrence to stealing, as also to gambling and swearing: 'it came into my head with a double force that this was the high-road to the devil, and that certainly this was not the life of a gentleman' (1, 76). This prevents him from becoming an abandoned criminal: he is never an instigator, often he is only a passive participant. It also prevents him from using his ill-gotten gains beyond the acquisition of necessities. He lodges his stolen money with a merchant and later has it sent after him to America, but the ship is lost and Jack does not actually enjoy the profits of crime. Throughout this early part of the novel Defoe shows a genuine compassion for destitute boys who are forced to steal by their undeserved condition; he insists, also, on the need for a good upbringing and a good education as preventives of delinquency. The transported and repentant criminal who in America becomes Jack's Tutor says to him:

> 'I believe my case was what I find is the case of most of the wicked part of the world, viz. that to be reduced

to necessity is not only the temptation, but is such a
temptation as human nature is not empowered to resist.
How good then,' says he, 'is that God which takes
from you, Sir, the temptation, by taking away the
necessity!' (1, 187)

After joining the army Jack is kidnapped and sent to Virginia
as a slave, a calamity which he looks upon as the workings of
Divine Providence, punishing him for his early wickedness,
although as yet he has no religious education. He becomes the
property of a kind master who makes him the overseer of the
Negroes, among whom Jack introduces gentle methods, instead of cruelty, in order to keep discipline in the plantation
and make them work.

By slow degrees Jack acquires his freedom, becomes a prosperous planter in his turn and is educated by the Tutor.
Leaving the latter in charge of his plantations, he returns to
Europe to live like a well-to-do gentleman and enters on
matrimonial adventures. His first wife, who is spendthrift and
adulterous, he divorces. She is later transported as a criminal
to Virginia where Jack finds her as one of his slaves. Like the
Tutor, like Jack himself, she there repents of her wicked life,
and Jack re-marries her. Defoe saw the plantations of Virginia
as the means of salvation for delinquents:

In a word, every Newgate wretch, every desperate for-
lorn creature, the most despicable ruined man in the
world, has here a fair opportunity put into his hands to
begin the world again, and that upon a foot of certain
gain and in a method exactly honest, with a reputation
that nothing past will have any effect upon; and in-
numerable people have raised themselves from the
worst circumstances in the world—namely, from the
cells in Newgate. (1, 178)

But the plantations are means to salvation only because they
are means to prosperity. Every transported felon, by being
given the opportunity to work, is given the opportunity of
ultimate ownership:

every year adding more land and planting more tobacco, which is real money, he must gradually increase in substance till at length he gets enough to buy negroes and other servants, and then never works himself any more. (1, 178)

From being a planter Jack becomes a trader and wealthy. And so, at the end, his thoughts, like Moll's, turn to religion. Conversion, which had been so real and important an element in the picaresque tradition, is now merely a literary and social convention – the adjunct to a respectable life, which has come to mean a prosperous one. Respectability had been attained by Guzmán on the torture-rack, by Simplicissimus in the cavern on the uninhabited island.

Colonel Jack is not, any more than *Moll Flanders*, a psychological or moral study of delinquency. At best it is only a sociological or 'economic' one. The picaresque tradition has moved away from a religious-moral preoccupation to humanitarianism. This is in no sense to be condemned in itself, but it constitutes a literary world of lower intellectual and emotional significance. Delinquency is treated by Defoe with a certain superficial optimism, which is a note alien to the Spanish picaresque tradition even in its decline. Castillo Solórzano is superficial, but his lack of any real interest in his delinquents does not extend to his being optimistic about their capacity for redemption. This optimism about life in general is more marked in France, where first the translators and then Lesage conjured away the serious moral and religious interest in delinquency that the Spanish *genre* had contained.

¶Little attention seems to be paid nowadays to the influence of the Spanish picaresque novel on French literature.[16] This is doubtless to be explained by the fact that Lesage, who alone really qualifies for inclusion under the category of picaresque,

[9.] Title-page of the first edition of *Moll Flanders* (see p. 100). The book was actually published in 1722, not in 1[7]21.

THE
FORTUNES
AND
MISFORTUNES
Of the FAMOUS
Moll Flanders, &c.

Who was Born in NEWGATE, and during a
Life of continu'd Variety for Threescore Years,
besides her Childhood, was Twelve Year a
Whore, five times a *Wife* (whereof once to her
own Brother) Twelve Year a *Thief*, Eight Year a
Transported *Felon* in *Virginia*, at last grew *Rich*,
liv'd *Honest*, and died a *Penitent*,

Written from her own MEMORANDUMS.

LONDON: Printed for, and Sold by W.
CHETWOOD, at *Cato's-Head*, in *Russel-
street, Covent-Garden*; and T. EDLING, at
the *Prince's-Arms*, over-against *Exerter-Change*
in the *Strand.* MDDCXXI.

Sorel, Scarron, and Furetière are so very different from the Spaniards that they can be thought to constitute a separate literary tradition on their own. One could even speak of French influence on the Spanish picaresque novel, since it has been remarked how different from the Spanish type—how much lighter and more amusing—are the three Spanish works from the picaresque canon that were published in France: *La desordenada codicia de los bienes ajenos* (Paris 1619) by Carlos García (*The Disordered Covetousness of Other Men's Goods*); *Segunda Parte de Lazarillo de Tormes* (Paris 1620) by H. de Luna (= Juan de Luna); and *Vida de Don Gregorio Guadaña* (Rouen 1644) by Antonio Enríquez Gómez.[17] None-the-less, in no other country did the Spanish novels enjoy as great a vogue in the seventeenth century as in France. This is evident from the number of translations and the number of their editions. Though neglected by histories of literature, these translations are historically of cardinal importance since they are the bridge between Alemán and Lesage and can alone explain the changes that the picaresque tradition underwent as it moved into the eighteenth century.

Lazarillo de Tormes was translated as early as 1561 and had five different translators up to 1678.[18] A translation by Gabriel Chappuys of the First Part of *Guzmán de Alfarache* appeared in Paris in 1600, the year after its publication in Spain; this was followed by translations by Jean Chapelain of Part 1 (*le Gueux, ou la Vie de Guzmán d'Alfarache*, Paris 1619) and of Part 11 in 1620. While in England there was only one translation of Alemán's novel, in France there were four in all, there being eighteen editions of the novel in French before the fourth version, by Lesage, appeared in 1732. There were twenty editions of *El buscón* in French during the seventeenth

---

[10.] Gil Blas becomes a country gentleman (see p. 122). He arrives with Scipion at the Château de Lirias and meets his servants. From the edition of Herman Uytwerf (Amsterdam 1727–35).

century in two different translations, *l'Aventurier Buscon, histoire facétieuse* (Paris 1633) by La Geneste, and in 1699 by Raclots, in *les Oeuvres de Don Francisco de Quevedo* (Brussels). In addition to these major works five lesser ones were translated up to 1661: *Marcos de Obregón*, by D'Audiguier in 1618, the same year as its publication in Spain; Luna's Second Part to *Lazarillo* (Paris 1620), and *La desordenada codicia* as *l'Antiquité des larrons* (Paris 1621), both also by D'Audiguier; *La pícara Justina* as *la Narquoise Justine* (Paris 1635); and Castillo Solórzano's *La garduña de Sevilla* as *la Fouine de Séville* (Paris 1661) by D'Ouville.

From the prefaces of the various translators one can discern two reasons for the extraordinary popularity of the Spanish *genre*. First, it satisfied the demand for a certain type of novelistic literature more effectively than the French themselves could. D'Audiguier in his *Lazarillo* (the original with Luna's continuation) of 1620 acknowledged that Spaniards were superior in the invention and construction of novels although they could not approach the French in purity of style.[19] But the quality in the Spanish works that was always singled out was their humour and irony. The first translation of *Lazarillo*, by Jean Saugrain (Paris 1561) had characterized it on the title-page as 'livre fort plaisant et délectable…en [lequel] l'esprit mélancolique se peut recréer et prendre plaisir'. *La pícara Justina* was of course classed with *Lazarillo* as 'plaisante', but we find it strange today that *Guzmán de Alfarache* was also: Jean-Pierre Camus, Bishop of Belley, wrote in the preface to his *Relations morales* (1631) that 'Guzman, Lazarille et la Justine sont des livres plutôt plaisants que sérieux'. This refusal (particularly by a bishop) to class *Guzmán* as 'serious' is an important sidelight on literary theory and fashion.

The second quality in the Spanish novels which appealed to French readers was their realism. Chapelain, in his translation of the First Part of *Guzmán* (1619), said that this novel had been received with acclamation all over Europe, being universally considered the best work of its kind, surpassing both its models, *The Golden Ass* and *Lazarillo*. Particularly excellent was the exact description of human malpractices ('les malversations du monde') and of the way in which men lived in every station in life, depicting all this with such precise detail that it left nothing to be desired. When he presented his translation of Part II he was even more lavish in his praise, calling it a 'precious jewel' as far superior to the First Part as the latter was to the false Second Part of 'Sayavedra'. This was because it portrayed an adult life ('toutes les rencontres vicieuses d'un homme en son âge viril') with admirable detail and an exact knowledge of all the abuses prevalent in society. He was thrilled by the subtlety of Guzmán's swindling: 'Tu y verras les fourbes les plus audacieuses, les coups plus hardis, les plus dommageables inventions.'[20]

What attracted, in short, was delinquency; but this was viewed from the comfortable security of an upper-class armchair as comedy. Charles Sorel in his *Bibliothèque française* (1664) included the French translations of Spanish picaresque novels among the *Romans comiques*, because they were characterized by truthfulness since they dealt with the common events of ordinary life. While Sorel admitted that not only beggars and thieves but many persons of quality could extract moral profit from *Guzmán de Alfarache*, he agreed with the criticism that found the moral discourses too long for that class of book.[21] Comic because realistic, realistic because comic: what appealed to the French public was the fact that these Spanish novels exemplified the 'low style' of literature. Nonethe-less, for all the translators without exception, the style of the Spaniards was too low. While praising the realism and the satire, they criticized the manner in which these were presented. Part II of *Guzmán*, said Chapelain, would be perfect if only the execution corresponded to the conception and invention; whereas, he complained, Alemán's style was not 'réglé': it lacked euphony, it was at times too laconic, at others too repetitive and had little syntactical and intellectual coherence.[22] Therefore, in order to make *Guzmán* acceptable,

Chapelain freely reconstructed the sentences, changed the metaphors, cut out whole sections and sometimes even added passages in order the better to link sentences or even incidents. Particularly significant is his contention that because Guzmán is a 'low' person his remarks ought to be ordinary, common and trivial; since this is, in fact, not so, Chapelain stated in his preface to Part II that he had tried to avoid as much as possible the elevated words and phrases that Alemán had put into his picaroon's mouth. Thereby he began, for purely 'literary' reasons, the process that later translators were to complete, that of purging *Guzmán* of all its digressions.

This was, of course, a conception of the art of translating very different from ours: it meant not rendering but 'improving' the originals, in order to make them conform to the standards and tastes of the new public. Chapelain affirmed that his object as a translator was not to reproduce all that was in the original but all in it that would please; he felt confident that he had made Alemán say all that he ought to have said, although there remained some passages where he had been compelled against his will to follow his author so as not to break the connexion with what had preceded. There is no point in our being superior about these liberties, despite the fact that with the irony of changes in fashion Alemán and Quevedo can nowadays be accepted as far finer stylists than their classically-minded translators. These translations are not so much blameworthy as, in fact, important practical illustrations of a theory of literature. This has been noted; what, however, has not been noted in any detail is their importance for the history of literature in connexion with the *genre* they exemplify. The 'improvements' of style meant that the tone of the originals was altered. Taking only our two main examples, *Guzmán de Alfarache* and *El buscón*, we find that the nervous strength, the intellectual agility, the idiomatic richness and the concreteness in the styles of Alemán and Quevedo are weakened into a looser, more evenly balanced, more urbane style, often with such a slackening of tension that the result tends to be commonplace. Lowering of tone and slackening of tension are evident also in the presentation of the plots. But despite its many changes, especially the abbreviation of many of the digressions, Chapelain's early version of *Guzmán* did not substantially alter the story. Two later French translations, which bring us into the age of Defoe, are, however, another matter.

In 1695 there appeared, first in Amsterdam and later in Paris, an *Histoire de l'admirable don Guzman d'Alfarache* without the names of author or translator; the latter was Sébastien Brémond.[23] In his anonymous preface he makes the customary claim to have brought the work closer to contemporary taste by deletions and additions, although he complains that this has by now become more difficult: 'Ce n'est pas une petite affaire, que d'un habit à l'espagnole en faire un à la française et surtout d'un habit vieux. L'antipatie de ces deux nations se trouve en tout.' He removes many of the digressions, although he adds others to satisfy his own animus against policemen and magistrates (according to Lesage he wrote his translation in prison). Among his deletions are most of the references to any religious feeling on Guzmán's part, and he removes entirely his repentance and conversion; which, of course, deprives the novel of its climax—in fact of its whole significance.

The fourth French translation of Alemán is the best known: *Histoire de Guzmán d'Alfarache, nouvellement traduite, et purgée des moralités superflues* (Paris 1732), by Alain René Lesage (1668–1747).[24] In his preface he censures Brémond for having distorted the original, not by what he omitted but by what he added. Lesage grants (significantly) that Alemán is too laconic in his comic scenes and that Brémond is right in principle to expand these, but states that he overdoes it; all his other additions are found blameworthy. Lesage's own translation, he claims, keep faithfully to Alemán's narrative. This fidelity takes the form of not adding anything but of omitting a very great deal. All the digressions disappear because this moralizing is superfluous, and Lesage follows Brémond in altering the ending. Guzmán's conversion is deleted, and with it the religious meditation that follows, his resistance to temptations and his constancy under trials; he is not tortured for alleged theft, only removed from the poop to the benches. Prior to this Lesage also deletes the periodic pangs of conscience to which Guzmán was subject. His version reduces the novel to the bare bones of the narrative by omitting not only the 'moralities' but all reference to religious feelings as well. Furthermore, Lesage makes Guzmán at the very end denounce the conspiracy of the galley-slaves, not in order to make right and justice prevail as is the case in Alemán, but in order to seek vengeance on the companion who had falsely accused him of stealing. For Lesage, Guzmán is a cynical cad to the very end. The meaning of the work is thus completely altered and Lesage does not warn his readers that this has happened. There is nothing underhand in this procedure; it is simply that the necessity for this 'improvement' was taken for granted, the probable reason being that religion was a subject to be treated 'seriously' and its association with the low world of the 'comic' was contrary to established taste. The dissociation was, of course, helped by the age's dislike of religious 'enthusiasm' and by a general weakening of the sense of sin.

The extent to which Lesage's *Guzmán* is a travesty of the original seems to have escaped notice, for I have not met any reference to the suppression of Guzmán's conscience and ultimate repentance and conversion. It has been too readily assumed that Lesage suppressed only what he stated he had suppressed, and that since these 'moralities' were 'superfluous' more good than harm had resulted. One critic, in fact, regretted that he did not go further and write an entirely new novel, so superior is his version to Alemán's.[25] Even today it is possible for Frenchmen who are not Hispanists to be apparently ignorant of the true ending that Alemán gave to his work.[26]

Brémond's translation was translated into English in 1707, purporting on the title-page to have been compared with the original.[27] This comparison did not extend to restoring the book's religious message or the hero's repentance. Lesage's translation was done into English by J.H. Brady in 1821, and reprinted in 1823 and 1881. Brady states that Lesage had omitted the 'superfluous reflections' of both Alemán and Brémond but does not state that he had tampered with the narrative. The 1881 edition is combined with a translation of *Lazarillo de Tormes* and contains a preface on the life of Alemán by Thomas Roscoe, the translator of *Lazarillo*[28]; not even he discloses what has happened to Alemán's work. Still another translation was made by Edward Lowdell, *The Amusing Adventures of Guzman de Alfaraque* [sic], (London 1883). The preface states: 'Following the example of Le Sage, the translator has sought to divest the work of the tedious and to modern notions misplaced disquisitions on morality and religion': what it does not state is that this is a translation of Lesage's version and not of the original. As for Lesage's translation itself, this was reprinted in France in the nineteenth century without the qualification on the title-page that it was 'purged of its superfluous moralizing' and without Lesage's preface–in short, with nothing whatever to prevent the reading public from taking it for granted that this was an accurate rendering of the original. Thus, for the whole of the eighteenth century and for most of the nineteenth, in both England and France, *Guzmán de Alfarache* appeared divorced from the moral-theological setting that alone gave meaning to the study of the delinquent's life.

What happened to *El buscón* in France is even more extraordinary. The translation by La Geneste (1633) was reprinted twenty times, either singly, or in editions of Quevedo's collected works, until 1699 when the version by Raclots appeared. This is actually La Geneste's version, only very slightly retouched.[29] La Geneste's translation contains a preface by the printer identifying the translator and adding that the translation has been fashioned in the French manner and 'marvellously embellished'.[30] The few scholars who refer to this translation[31] all note that the novel has been completed by making Pablos fall in love with a rich merchant's daughter and marry her, thus leading him to a prosperous and reformed life. But none of them note that this is an ending that does not merely replace Quevedo's final paragraph; it replaces the whole closing section of the novel including the climax, which entirely disappears. Even prior to this various changes are introduced that make it impossible from this translation to detect the psychological analysis I outlined above. For instance, in the passages quoted on pages 64 and 65 above, the incident of Pablos learning his lesson well to please the master and receiving a reward in consequence is omitted; his unsolicited running of errands for the master's wife is turned into her selecting him for this task because of his vivaciousness; his self-identification with his mother's guilt in the 'Cock King' episode is suppressed. The second half of Chapter XIX[32] and the whole of Chapter XX are omitted, namely his posing as a gentleman, his successful courting of an heiress, his exposure and punishment. The translation is resumed with Chapter XXI, but ceases before Pablos becomes a 'Convent gallant' in Chapter XXII[33]; the whole of the last chapter (XXIII) is omitted. What disappears with these extensive cuts is all Pablos's major delinquency–his imposture, his final association with gangsters, his implication in a murder, and his being hounded by the police–in short, everything in his career that borders on the criminal. With his being thus promoted to an entertaining adventurer, the stage is set for the new ending.

Quevedo's ending, it will be recalled, leaves Pablos on the point of embarking for America in order to escape the police, with a hint that his fortunes would none-the-less go from bad to worse. This ending, or lack of ending, by making the story of Pablos's delinquent career peter out into nothingness, is perfectly in keeping with the psychology of the delinquent as Quevedo presents it and with the satirical technique he devised for expressing it. But this 'unfinished' ending was–not in itself surprisingly–unacceptable to La Geneste. What kind of ending was he to give it? If he were to follow up Quevedo's closing comment, if, in fact, he were to carry the theme to the logical conclusion to which Quevedo's treatment pointed, he would have to give it a tragic ending. But is it not a satirical and therefore a comic work, an 'histoire facétieuse'? It must therefore be given a happy ending, and so where Quevedo makes Pablos's fortunes decline, La Geneste makes them rise. In Quevedo, Pablos's desire from childhood to become a gentleman is an ambition that he is under a compulsion to achieve in order to escape from his burden of social guilt and shame. Since he can only achieve this ambition by fraud, it is the motivating force behind his deliberate choice of delinquency. Everything therefore leads up to the climax of his imposture, after which everything leads down to the petering-out of his now negative existence. Abandoning his text before the climax that precipitates the decline, La Geneste makes Pablos a successful actor, who is able to save a considerable sum of money; moving to Seville he falls in love with a rich girl whose beautiful face he sees at the window; he becomes a servant in her house, lets drop a false letter addressed to himself as a Knight of St James; spins a romantic story about a quarrel at court that requires him to remain incognito, and assures her he has become a servant only to further his love. Her mother, when informed of this, is only too happy to consent to her daughter's marriage to so great a gentleman. After the marriage he confesses to his wife the trick he has played on her, but she is too much in love with him to mind. The bride's father, who all this time has been conveniently in America, is drowned at sea; the mother dies of a broken heart and Pablos, with no one to hold his imposture against him, settles down to the comfortable life of a rich man, thus achieving his childhood's ambition.

Everything that constitutes the brilliant originality of *El buscón* thus disappears. The tragedy and suffering of the delinquent, his symbolical refusal to take up his Cross, his seeking revenge on society for his own shame, are watered down

and become undetectable by being deprived of their fulfilment and by being turned into a trivial success story of the
poor boy who makes good. This is the degradation of a masterpiece. French neo-classicism had to reimpose the barrier
between the comic and the serious which the Spaniards had
in part removed. Because *Guzmán de Alfarache* was realistic
it could not be serious; its moral and religious interests had
therefore eventually to be eliminated. Because *El buscón* was
comic it had to have a happy ending; all that made its delinquent protagonist undeserving of success and prosperity had
therefore to be eliminated.

La Geneste's *Buscon* is the precedent for the delinquents
who become prosperous and respectable in the novels of
Defoe, for it was translated into English in 1657 (republished
in 1670) by John Davies of Kidwelly with no indication that
it did not come from the Spanish and was not a faithful repro-
duction of the original.[34] One must expect Gil Blas to follow
suit, for the same spirit was at work in Lesage when he turned
to handle picaresque material of his own accord. The *Histoire
de Gil Blas de Santillane* (1715, 1724, and 1735) is, in fact,
vastly different from the genuine *Guzmán de Alfarache* and
the genuine *Buscón*. We find formal qualities that Alemán and
Quevedo do not possess: an elegant air, an urbane neatness of
style, a gentle humour, a restrained and sometimes pleasing
irony, coupled with a power of exact observation and an eye
for realistic detail devoid of exaggeration. These qualities,
which certainly make for easier reading, bring with them a
subdued and mellowed portrayal of the world of the picaresque.
Spaniards of the eighteenth century were able to be convinced
by Voltaire that *Gil Blas* was really a translation of an unknown
Spanish novel which Lesage had discovered in manuscript,
but no Spaniard of Alemán's generation, or of Quevedo's,
would have recognized in it a familiar literary world. So un-
Spanish is it that it is hard to believe that this controversy was
ever taken seriously.

From the very start Gil Blas is dissociated from his Spanish prototypes by being the product of a respectable milieu. The son of decent lower middle-class parents, he receives a reasonable education, and he leaves home not to seek freedom from discipline but to attend the University. That he never gets there is not his fault: it is the result purely of mischance. Once set on the path of ill luck he travels through the country tossed between adversity and good fortune. No sooner is he rewarded than he is cheated, for he is inexperienced and trusting, and so easy game for confidence tricksters. Roguery exists not in him but in the world outside him. But although this roguery embraces brigands who not only steal but murder, these delinquents are good-humoured and everything is done and described in a gentlemanly and restrained manner: we are amused, not shocked, much less disturbed.

Gil Blas is thus, in his formative years, not a responsible moral agent but, to use the expression he comes to apply to himself, 'the plaything of fortune'. If he begins to lose moral scruples where money is concerned, this is an excusable opportunism, an endeavour to make the best of events while being dogged by a persistent bad luck that has impoverished him undeservedly. Destitution compels him to become a servant instead of a student, and while the ups and downs continue they do so in a gradual ascent to success and prosperity. From being the servant of a priest, he becomes secretary to an archbishop, then on to being secretary to no less a person than the Duke of Lerma, Chief Minister of the Crown. In this position he is not only close to affairs of State but associates with royalty. This is the most astonishing transformation in the whole history of the picaresque *genre*, which has by now come to foster the aristocratic cult of propriety, decorum and social gentility in literature. What has traditionally been called Lesage's 'universalization' of the picaresque is in reality only its 'aristocratization'. The delinquency in Gil Blas's environment also ascends the social ladder and becomes political favouritism, the acceptance of bribes, and pandering to the amours of the heir to the throne. Even this sort of corruption is good-natured, and although the hero's implication in the Prince's illicit love affair lands him in prison, it is only to enable him to repent and to learn the last lesson of experience, which is the charm of country life. His repentance comes, like that of Moll Flanders, when, falling seriously ill, he thinks he is faced with death. This makes him despise wealth and worldly honours, and he determines, when cured of his illness and released from prison, to buy a small cottage with the money that remains to him and to live a simple and frugal life. But he is saved from a fate that promises to be little better than the hermitage of Simplicissimus, and his disenchantment is given a reward more in keeping with the values of the new age, when he meets again Don Alphonse de Leyva, one of his former masters for whom he had obtained from Lerma the 'governor-ship' of Valencia. Don Alphonse bestows on Gil Blas the estate of Lirias, which produces an income of five hundred ducats a year.

This is the end of Volume III (1724). The last volume, comprising Books X–XII, was published in 1735. Here Gil Blas is given the chance to redeem his disgrace. At Lirias he had married, but his wife died after giving birth to a son. A new reign has started, and now that the Prince he had served is Philip IV, he returns to seek favour at Court. Becoming secretary to Lerma's successor, the Count-Duke Olivares, Gil Blas shows that he can now handle power without serving his own interests; instead, he makes himself useful to friends and benefactors. When Olivares falls he accompanies him into exile and eventually, rejecting the advice to live in penitential retirement in a religious house, he returns to his 'more agree-able' rural retreat (Book XII, cap. xii), where he achieves at last the ideal of an eighteenth-century gentleman: he cultivates sensibility and tender feelings, is responsive to the beauty of nature and the beauty of poetry, reads the classical authors and the moral philosophers, and experiences the joys of marriage and fatherhood. Thus, in the long run, the good always gets the better of the bad.

This optimism not only colours the final prosperity and happiness of Gil Blas, it is of course what, from the very start, had coloured the whole presentation of a society in which delinquency ostensibly plays a large part. We can afford to take it lightly and good-humouredly, because, after all, everything is for the best, if not in the best of all possible worlds, at least in a world that is not really as bad as we might think. One is no longer surprised after reading *Gil Blas* that Lesage did not care for Alemán's sermonizing. One suspects that it was not only his classical dislike of mixing seriousness with the comedy of the low style that made him unable to stomach, and certainly unable to handle, strong or serious emotion. The brief description of the repentance of Gil Blas is sufficient illustration of this inability:

> I was therefore expecting to cross the bar; none the less this expectation proved mistaken. Since my doctors had abandoned me, they left nature in possession of the field; thereby they saved my life. The fever, which according to their diagnosis ought to have carried me off, left me as if in order to prove them wrong. By the greatest good fortune I recovered little by little; a perfect tranquillity of mind became the fruit of my illness. I had no need then of consolation. I had for riches and for honours all the contempt that the prospect of approaching death had made me feel; and having thus found myself, I blessed my misfortune. I thanked heaven for it as for a special grace it had given me; and I made a firm resolve never more to return to Court even if the Duke of Lerma were to summon me back. Instead I proposed, if I ever left prison, to buy a cottage and to live like a philosopher in it.[35]

Neither the sentiment nor the tone is really serious. The commonplace, perfunctory nature of this repentance, especially when compared with Guzmán's, is the measure of Lesage's attitude to delinquency, since this is how he presents its rejection.

Nor in the wider context of novelistic art is anything gained by the elevation of the Spanish picaroon to the ranks of the aristocracy. Neither in its style nor in its 'philosophy' has the novel much to commend it. Its wit never has the bite and pungency, nor the brilliant word-play, of a Quevedo.[36] The passage just quoted bears out Vivienne Mylne's contention that Lesage's

> major defect as a novelist may well be precisely that cool
> and level style for which he is so frequently praised.
> Its cumulative effect is a uniformity, an evenness,
> which spreads over great and small events alike, and
> flattens what might be a mountainous landscape into a
> mere plateau. In this uniformity the climactic events
> are lost, and the shape of the plot with them.[37]

As for the 'philosophy', there is not even the compensation of Defoe's humanitarianism. The fact that the novel teaches no deeper lesson than that we should not make fools of ourselves used to be considered its strength, since the aim of comic writing is to amuse, not to improve. Nowadays, however, its admirers see rather more in this lesson. *Gil Blas*, it is held, is based on two contradictory ideas: there is on the one hand the satire that sees the world as a stage and life as an illusory play-acting, and on the other hand the constructive aspect of the theme whereby life is shown to be worth living because it 'forms man', who comes to find himself only after an arduous and circuitous journey. The coherent theme that emerges out of these contradictions is said to be an original conception of man's estate.[38] What exactly is original in the trivial statement that we learn from experience is not clear. Even less convincing is the attempt to make Lesage's view of human life a pessimistic one in that the wisdom Gil Blas arrives at in prison – and the moral of the whole work – rejects wealth and possessions for being the sources of moral corruption: 'Les biens ne sont propres qu'à corrompre mes mœurs', says Gil Blas to Don Alphonse as he refuses the latter's offer of money (after having, one should add, accepted the offer of the estate with its

revenue). This moral, it is alleged, is what differentiates Gil
Blas from his Spanish picaresque forebears and from the
heroes of the French 'romans comiques', since they cling as
best they can to such material prosperity as their moral opportunism has brought them.[39] To detect any renunciation, in
any deep moral sense, in *Gil Blas* is laughable; not to detect
it in Alemán (or Grimmelshausen) is unpardonable. Yet the
upward progress of Gil Blas towards prosperity is also attributed to the influence of the Spanish picaresque novels, since
Lazarillo 'became a town-crier' (and a complacent cuckold!),
Guzmán 'the favourite of the captain of a galley' (but a galley-
slave after having been a prosperous merchant!), and Pablos
'is on the point of emigrating to America' (but to escape from
the police; and in America 'things were to go worse' for
him!).[40] The attempt to base Lesage's 'morality of success'
(*Erfolgsmoral*) on the Spanish picaresque tradition cannot be
allowed to stand.

In passing from Alemán, Quevedo and Grimmelshausen to
Lesage, *via* the French translations, the literature of delinquency has in fact turned a somersault. The reform of Gil
Blas, and the optimistic 'disenchantment' that motivates his
withdrawal to the prosperous life of a country gentleman,
would have aroused in all three a sardonic laughter. The only
optimism Grimmelshausen could feel lay in the possibility of
eremitical solitude away from the warfare of human life. The
only optimism Alemán could feel was belief in divine grace:
if this is an illusion, he would have said, then there are no
grounds for hoping that the delinquent can ever cease to be.
As regards Quevedo, the question of optimism or pessimism
is altogether too crude for the level on which he presents delinquency – that of the suffering endured by a man who is an
outsider because of a burden of shame and guilt too heavy to
be borne without resentment and revenge. By comparison
with these three predecessors, the originality of Lesage within
his tradition is only a descent to the superficial and the commonplace.

¶After Lesage the only European novelist of any importance in whom the Spanish picaresque tradition is still recognizable is Tobias Smollett (1721–71). His novels, it has been asserted, 'bear the stamp of Spanish picaresque fiction…. There is probably no Spanish author Smollett more resembles than certain works of Quevedo, in matter, though not in style. From Quevedo's *Life of Paul the Great Rascal* to Smollett's *Roderick Random* is not a big step.'[41] On the contrary, there is an abyss. The alleged resemblance lies probably in the cruelty, the ruthless realism and the scatological features of both novels.

Smollett himself confesses, in his preface to *Roderick Random* (1748), that his model was *Gil Blas*.[42] Roderick is, however, no delinquent, and his life-story cannot really be called a picaresque novel; in this respect it opens still further the gap between its French model and the Spanish sources. None-the-less, Smollett deliberately lays more stress on the wickedness of the world, asserting that Lesage has gone too far in the direction of comedy:

> The disgraces of Gil Blas are, for the most part, such as rather excite mirth than compassion; he himself laughs at them; and his transitions from distress to happiness, or at least ease, are so sudden, that neither the reader has time to pity him, nor himself to be acquainted with affliction. This conduct, in my opinion, not only deviates from probability, but prevents that generous indignation which ought to animate the reader against the sordid and vicious disposition of the world.

> I have attempted to represent modest merit struggling with every difficulty to which a friendless orphan is exposed, from his own want of experience, as well as from *the selfishness, envy, malice, and base indifference of mankind*. [The italics are mine.]

The wickedness, therefore, is not in the hero but in the men he meets. Although there are Spanish precedents, notably *Marcos de Obregón*, this of itself is very unpicaresque. Roderick's 'modest merit' means a good, generous disposition and a quickness to come to the help of others; it also means a righteous indignation at injustice. Apart from the callous exploitation of the faithful Strap, whose modest fortune he has no qualms in squandering, the only action of Roderick's that approaches delinquency (and it is in the direct tradition of *El buscón*) is his attempt to palm himself off on a rich heiress as a young man of wealth. He later tells her that he would never have actually carried through the deception by marrying on it, but he is prepared at the time to act the lie. In contrast to the 'meritorious' hero, the world around him is remarkably cruel. Men are not just villainous, they are totally heartless and indifferent to brutality. Captain Oakhum and Dr Mackshane, to mention only two, are brutal bullies for no apparent reason at all—they merely happen to be such. There is the harrowing story of the dramatic poet, the good and gentle Melopoyn, reduced to nakedness and starvation in the debtors' prison by the failure of his patrons to fulfil their promises. Roderick comments that they were 'a set of scoundrels, who were so habituated to falsehood and equivocation, that I verily believe that they would have found the utmost difficulty in uttering one syllable of truth, though their lives depended upon their sincerity' (cap. XXVIII). But these 'scoundrels' do not profit in any way from their falsehood, they derive no advantage whatsoever from duping Melopoyn. They merely represent the perfidy of 'the world', which is itself so pointless that one cannot help feeling it to be merely a personal resentment on the part of the author. The novel is in no sense an exploration of human delinquency.

The Adventures of Ferdinand Count Fathom (1753) is not one of Smollett's successful novels, but it is the only one that is fully picaresque—the last European novel of any consequence that is directly within the tradition started by *Guzmán de Alfarache*.[43] The preface echoes the statement Alemán had made of his intentions:

Let me not, therefore, be condemned for having chosen

my principal character from the purlieus of treachery
and fraud, when I declare my purpose is to set him up
as a beacon for the benefit of the unexperienced and un-
wary, who, from the perusal of these memoirs, may
learn to avoid the manifold snares with which they are
continually surrounded in the paths of life; while those
who hesitate on the brink of iniquity may be terrified
from plunging into that irremediable gulf by surveying
the deplorable fate of *Ferdinand Count Fathom*.

El buscón has been claimed as Smollett's direct source.[44] Although he cannot approach Quevedo's sardonic wit, there are
some episodes, such as Fathom's first visit to prison (cap.
XXXIX–XLI), where we find scenes and meet characters (like
Captain Minikin, Major Macleaver, Sir Mungo Barebones,
King Theodore of Corsica) that have a grotesqueness not
altogether unworthy of the Spanish master. But the influence
of *El buscón* is to be found in the general pattern rather than
in any particular details. First, there is the disreputable
mother: a prostitute hanger-on of an army, who roams the
battlefields, murdering the wounded in order to plunder them
as well as the already dead. Secondly, there is the fact that
Fathom is befriended by a noble family and grows up as the
companion of the son, Renaldo Count Melvil, who is the
counterpart of Don Diego. Thirdly, there is the university to
which Fathom accompanies his aristocratic friend. But there
the influence of *El buscón* ceases.

A consummate hypocrite from boyhood, Fathom grows into
an unmitigated scoundrel; but he possesses good looks, a
charm of manner which he knows how to exploit, learning
and wit; he is also a consummate musician, able to enchant all
listeners with his violin. He is suave and polite, but utterly unscrupulous as a thief, a swindler and a deceiver of women.
Smollett breaks with the picaresque tradition by making
Fathom a delinquent from the very start; he does not develop
into one; it is just his 'humour'. He is the 'type' of ruthless
egoist, a constitutional delinquent, one predisposed to this be-

haviour because of the physical or mental constitution with which he was born. In short, unlike every picaroon from Guzmán to Gil Blas, he is the primitive type of literary villain. No explanation is offered for his character; it undergoes no development until after fifty-five chapters, when he is faced with ruin from which there is no escape and which will land him in prison for bankruptcy. This is the situation of Guzmán and Moll Flanders, except that Fathom's conversion precedes his actual imprisonment:

Such a concurrence of sinister events made a deep impression upon the mind of our adventurer. All his fortitude was insufficient to bear him up against this torrent of misfortune; his resources were all dried up, his invention failed, and his reflection began to take a new turn. 'To what purpose', said he to himself, 'have I deserted the paths of integrity and truth, and exhausted a fruitful imagination, in contriving schemes to betray my fellow-creatures, if, instead of acquiring a splendid fortune, which was my aim, I have suffered such a series of mortifications, and at last brought myself to the brink of inevitable destruction? By a virtuous exertion of those talents I inherit from nature and education, I might, long before this time, have rendered myself independent, and, perhaps, conspicuous in life.

After passing his crimes in review, he continues:

Shall the author of these crimes pass with impunity? Shall he hope to prosper in the midst of such enormous guilt? It were an imputation upon Providence to suppose it! Ah, no! I begin to feel myself overtaken by the eternal justice of Heaven! I totter on the edge of wretchedness and woe, without one friendly hand to save me from the terrible abyss! (cap. LVI)

Vice has not paid; virtue probably would have done. Any swindler to whom dishonesty has not brought success will turn to honesty if he thinks it will better his fortune; but this is a change of tactics, not of heart. Yet Smollett says of Fathom that 'no sinner underwent such severe remorse as that which he suffered during his imprisonment' (cap. LXVII). Since Fathom is not given the chance to see whether virtue will in fact make him 'conspicuous in life', his conversion is intended to be sincere and not a matter of expediency. This makes it even less convincing than that of Moll Flanders, for her return to virtue is an opportunism that corresponds to the improvement in her circumstances, whereas Fathom's, being 'genuine', reflects ostensibly an inner transformation for which the ground has not, however, been prepared. Unlike Guzmán or Simplicissimus there is no single trait in his character that could at any time have pointed in this direction. His conversion is therefore just as unaccountable as his delinquency. Alemán, Quevedo, and Grimmelshausen could never have been guilty of such novelistic irresponsibility, for it was not in their age to permit it.

Smollett presented an unexplained conversion on top of an unexplained delinquency in order to conform to the fashion of his age by making Fathom deserve the magnanimity of the three persons whom he had most outrageously wronged – Monimia, whom he had driven to a supposed death, Renaldo and Diego de Zelos, both of whom he had driven to destitution. Between Fathom's change of heart in cap. LVI and his reappearance in cap. LXVII, the novel changes from a picaresque narrative to a sentimental romance as his three victims return to prosperity and happiness. Instead of seeking vengeance on Fathom, they not only forgive him but rescue him from certain death in destitution by giving him a country dwelling and an annuity, which enable him to live, although more modestly, in respectable retirement like Moll Flanders, Colonel Jack, and Gil Blas. This is the 'deplorable fate' which Smollett in his preface hoped would scare away those hesitating on the 'brink of iniquity'.

From delinquent to country gentleman – even Fathom is not an exception to this eighteenth-century rule. This humanitarianism had not been felt by the seventeenth century, to the detriment of its social life but to the benefit of its literature. The sentiment is not, of course, to be derided in itself, but in *Count Fathom* it is presented naïvely and in the context of a sentimental melodrama. When Moll Flanders turns to virtue in time of prosperity, Defoe is being not only more realistic but also more healthy, for Smollett's humanitarianism is greatly weakened by its remarkably lachrymose setting, the second half of the novel being a bad example of the tearful sensibility that is the least significant characteristic of eighteenth-century literature. It is still further weakened by not being devoid of self-interest. 'Renaldo honestly owned that, exclusive of other reasons, he could not deny himself the luxurious enjoyment of communicating happiness to his fellow-creatures in distress; and each fervently prayed, that their charity might not be disappointed by the death of the object' (cap. LXVII); that is, they prayed that Fathom might not succumb to his illness.

While the main picaresque tradition thus undergoes decline in England at the hands of Defoe and Smollett, parallel to its decline in France, the literature of delinquency in its burlesque form reaches its peak with *The Life of Mr Jonathan Wild the Great* (1743) by Henry Fielding (1707–54). What most differentiates Fielding from Smollett–his geniality, good nature and humaneness–is what removes him from the sphere of the picaresque and allies him with Cervantes, his acknowledged master. *Tom Jones* should not be included among picaresque novels, for its hero is no delinquent but a youth of generous and open character: although he is lax and imprudent there is no pride, meanness or revengefulness in him. Jonathan Wild is a delinquent, but his story is not, properly speaking, a picaresque novel either, despite the fact that *The Spanish Rogue* is stated to be his favourite book (Book I, cap. iii); it is a skit on the English criminal biographies which are an offshoot from, rather than part of, the direct line that goes from *Guzmán de Alfarache* to *Count Fathom*. Its Spanish precedent is *La pícara Justina*; the similarity between the two works, which is purely coincidental, lies in the fact that both parody the serious treatment of a literary subject that they consider ought to be treated light-heartedly or sarcastically. Jonathan Wild was one of the real-life criminals that the English pamphlets held up for praise as heroic and 'great' men. Fielding holds Wild up for mock praise as the symbol of human greatness, and he sustains the irony and banter without flagging. The tone is often embarrassing, especially when it veers into sentimentality with the treatment of Heartfree and his wife, who are the 'good' counterparts to the 'great' Wild. It also becomes tiresome as the 'Great Man' is ironically extolled on every page. None-the-less, the style is infinitely superior to the crude frivolity of *La pícara Justina*. The irony often conveys a wit that is pointed with a politico-social relevance:

> The day of his trial now approached; for which, as Socrates did, he prepared himself; but not weakly and foolishly, like that philosopher, with patience and resignation; but with a good number of false witnesses. However, as success is not always proportioned to the wisdom of him who endeavours to attain it; so are we more sorry than ashamed to relate that our hero was, notwithstanding his utmost caution and prudence, convicted, and sentenced to a death, which, when we consider, not only the Great Men who have suffered it, but the much larger number of those whose highest honour it hath been to merit it, we cannot call otherwise than honourable. Indeed those, who have unluckily missed it, seem all their days to have laboured in vain to attain an end, which Fortune, for reasons only known to herself, hath thought proper to deny them. (Book IV, cap. xiii)

The political barb is, of course, new to the picaresque tradition:

> With such infinite address did this truly Great Man know how to play with the passions of men, and to set them

at variance with each other, and to work his own purposes out of those jealousies and apprehensions, which
he was wonderfully ready at creating, by means of those
great arts, which the vulgar call Treachery, Dissembling,
Promising, Lying, Falsehood, etc., but which are by
Great Men summed up in the collective name of Policy,
or Politics, or rather Pollitricks; an Art of which, as it
is the highest excellence of human nature, so perhaps
was our Great Man the most eminent master. (Book II,
cap. v)

Jonathan Wild is in no sense a study of delinquency and does not
aim to be one; delinquency in it is the means to a wider end.
It does not therefore invalidate the conclusion that the eighteenth century did not present a significant literary treatment
of delinquency from the directly realistic angle. The strength
of the age, in the general sphere of a social-moral literature,
lay rather in irony and satire. *Gulliver's Travels* and *Candide*,
as well as *Jonathan Wild*, are proof of this.

¶One might go further and say that the eighteenth century
could not present a significant literary treatment of delinquency.
The difference between the conversions of Guzmán and Simplicissimus on the one hand, and of Moll Flanders, Colonel
Jack, and Gil Blas on the other, is to be explained not only as
the rise of the new capitalism; it is also the difference between
two opposing sets of moral values. In 1751 David Hume defined virtue as 'the possession of mental qualities, *useful* or
agreeable to the *person himself* or to *others*', and stated that no
other definition

will ever be received, where men judge of things by their
natural, unprejudiced reason, without the delusive
glosses of superstition and false religion. Celibacy, fast-
ing, penance, mortification, self-denial, humility, silence,
solitude [i.e. the virtues implicitly or explicitly upheld
by Alemán and Grimmelshausen], and the whole train
of monkish virtues; for what reason are they everywhere

rejected by men of sense, but because they serve to no manner of purpose; neither advance a man's fortune in the world, nor render him a more valuable member of society; neither qualify him for the entertainment of company, nor increase his power of self-enjoyment? We observe, on the contrary, that they cross all these desirable ends; stupify the understanding and harden the heart, obscure the fancy and sour the temper. We justly, therefore, transfer them to the opposite column, and place them in the catalogue of vices; nor has any superstition force sufficient among men of the world to prevent entirely these natural sentiments.[45]

The seventeenth century could have objected that while mortification, self-denial and humility certainly did not advance a man's fortune in the world, their absence could lead to the delinquency that would be the chosen means for such an advance. Precisely because ' "respectability", the virtue of standing well with one's neighbours, becomes, in [Hume's] kind of world, the *summum bonum*',[46] the repentant delinquents of Defoe and Lesage are transformed into well-to-do owners of property. Delinquency, for their age, was an aberration that would disappear with a comfortable income and with the general growth of humanitarian feeling (the 'useful' to 'others'). Two centuries later our society has not proved this true, since the modern 'unattached' who find an outlet in delinquency have generally plenty of money to spend and live in a Welfare State. It is a spectacular fact that in our day 'a steep and steady rise in the standard of living of practically all social classes in Western Europe and the Americas has been accompanied by a steep and steady rise in the rate of crimes, including all forms of property'.[47]

A man or boy threatened with hunger and destitution will of course steal, as Defoe knew. In Spain the author of *Lazarillo de Tormes* knew it too, although what he wished to emphasize was not the consequent formation of delinquent habits but the fact that, in the long run, this stealing from necessity could weaken the sense of personal honour. In *Guzmán de Alfarache* and *El buscón* stealing occurs only after delinquent habits have been formed for other reasons; in *Simplicissimus* there is the disorderly influence of a riotous, chaotic, and cruel environment. In all three novels delinquency is a form of self-assertion in the young that seeks approbation from companions and that is fanned by praise and flattery. In short, delinquency is pride, a disorder in the individual will that in modern terms can be called 'the will to power' but that the seventeenth century knew as Original Sin, a disorder that makes the adjustment of the will to the conscience difficult in face of the urge to freedom and independence. In *Simplicissimus* this same disorder is presented in human society rather than in the individual, and the sign of it is war, which is the delinquency of men against their own nature as social beings. In two of these novels religion emerges as the loyalty to something higher than itself that humanity needs to profess in order to kill the urge to delinquency. If May has correctly detected and interpreted the symbolism of *El buscón*, this loyalty is there too, implicitly; but with or without it, deliberate pride is explicitly presented as the motive for delinquency after the influence of environment has created the predisposition. In all three novels the reader is involved by his common humanity in the pessimism or disenchantment. In Defoe the reader is involved by a humanitarian sense of compassion for the unfortunate, but once the misfortune is removed by prosperity sympathy is no longer called for. In Smollett a 'constitutional' delinquency is overcome by humanitarian sentiments of charitableness, the reader is involved only by the flattering of his sense of superiority—it is more pleasurable, more self-satisfying, to reward than to punish. In Lesage the reader is not involved in any way: the comfortable basis of an aristocratic society is never really threatened, and the reader can sit back secure and be amused.

The eighteenth century was an unquestionably great age in our civilization, but it was great only in certain things and in certain ways—in its rationalism, reasonableness, good sense; its spirit of scientific enquiry and experiment; its sense of order and propriety; its hatred of superstition, of intolerant authority, and of tyranny. All these things together bred a sense of progress and a spirit of optimism that led to the great movement of liberalism. But it was precisely this spirit of optimism and the scientific rationalism which engendered it that, by being, in literature, hostile to a sense of suffering, tended to make the age insensitive to the concept of guilt and to any existential anguish—insensitive also to the awareness of evil that had made the age of Shakespeare the age of great tragedy. Guilt, existential anguish, suffering, and tragedy are at the heart of delinquency—of the delinquency of the individual against society, of the delinquency of mankind against God. The age of Shakespeare could feel these things and ponder them in a way that the age of Lesage could not. *Guzmán de Alfarache* and *El buscón* could focus with acuteness of insight and intensity of feeling the problem of delinquency, and *Simplicissimus* could follow them in this because it was born out of the anguish and suffering of a whole nation.

But with the turn of the new century, the literature of delinquency was bound to take on quite a different tone. Suffering and anguish became suspect; it was thought that the sense of tragedy should be removed from existence by removing religious zeal and the fear of damnation. Religion thus tended to become a question of 'good nature'. Shaftesbury would have disliked the religious note in *Guzmán de Alfarache* and in *Simplicissimus* because it was 'melancholy' and therefore tragic; on the other hand, he would have approved of Moll Flanders's piety, based as it was on a practical good humour. Brémond and Lesage banned religion from *Guzmán de Alfarache* when they translated it, because it was unseemly to associate religion with the sinful. In any case morality had to be made independent of religion: when Gil Blas is converted from the corruption of political life, he embraces the new morality of the *honnêtes gens*—a psychological morality, based on a civilized rationality. Man might still in theory be suspended between heaven and hell, but in literature itself he was no longer struggling up to the one or sinking down to the other; instead, human fulfilment was to be found in the bourgeois comforts of a reasonable income.

Enlightenment was not, of course, absent from the moral and social principles of the eighteenth century; this notwithstanding, it was an age in which society did not, and in fact could not, incite the writer to examine at all deeply the image of the delinquent. The underlying tensions of Baroque culture could do precisely this, as can the tensions of our own world today. The three great picaresque novels, *Guzmán de Alfarache*, *El buscón*, and *Simplicissimus* are far more modern than Defoe and Lesage. Vivienne Mylne rightly maintains that Lesage cannot offer us either enrichment of experience or insight into the human predicament, and that for novels that can offer this we must move forward to Balzac and his successors.[48] One must, of course, agree; but one should add that we can also look back to Grimmelshausen, to Quevedo, to Alemán (and of course to Cervantes). The history of the European novel is not a steady rise from *Lazarillo de Tormes* to Defoe and Lesage and on to Balzac. In what primarily makes novels significant as mirrors of human life—in intellectual depth, psychological insight, and moral awareness—Defoe and Lesage represent depressions when compared with the best of what had gone before. The history of the modern European novel should be rewritten with a truer perspective.

APPENDIX

The Alleged Unorthodoxy of 'Guzmán de Alfarache'

On page 31 above it was asserted that the quotations from *Guzmán de Alfarache* which J. A. van Praag adduces as evidence of a mocking, sarcastic, or cynical attitude to Catholic doctrine and practices, are misinterpreted by him through unfamiliarity with Catholic usage and tradition, disregard of the non-literal character of some Spanish idioms, disregard of the context, and a failure to distinguish cases where the author speaks in character from those where he speaks in person. It would be as tedious as it is unnecessary to examine each one of van Praag's instances of alleged unorthodoxy. Examples are selected under each of these headings to show the ways in which they are misinterpreted.

[1] *Disregard of figurative usage.* In Spain, perhaps more than in other Roman Catholic countries, religious expressions have become idioms or stock phrases and are used with a familiarity that it would astonish Spaniards to hear called irreverent: for instance, '¡Jesús!' used when someone sneezes, to express the hope that he is not getting a cold (cf. the proverb: 'Cuando Francia estornuda, España dice Jesús'); or 'andar de Herodes a Pilatos' as the equivalent of 'out of the frying-pan into the fire'. Van Praag tends to assume that such expressions denote an ironical attitude to the religious practices they refer to. When Guzmán has been the victim of a practical joke on

the part of a young woman who, after inviting him into her house, had put him inside a big jar because her so-called brother had arrived, he leaves the house 'haciendo cruces a las esquinas con determinación de nunca volverlas a cruzar'.[1] For van Praag this pokes fun at the practice of crossing oneself. There is, of course, a punning joke on 'cruzar', but 'hacer cruces a' is an established phrase for to take definite leave of something (that is, giving a parting blessing). In the same way crossing oneself has become a normal way of expressing surprise; yet van Praag takes it to be a mockery of religious practice when Alemán thus describes Guzmán's skill in stealing carefully guarded objects: 'Santiguábase monseñor, maravillado cómo pudiera ser. En cuanto acabó de comer y alzaron la mesa, no hacía otra cosa que santiguarse con toda la mano' (II, 271). In *Don Quijote*, when the astonished Sancho sees the face of the defeated Sansón Carrasco, Cervantes writes: 'Llegó Sancho, y como miró el rostro del Bachiller Carrasco, comenzó a hacerse mil cruces y a santiguarse otras tantas' (Part II, cap. xiv).

[2] *Unfamiliarity with Catholic tradition.* Alemán wrote: 'Como el hombre sea perfeto animal racional, criado para eternidad, semejante a Dios, como él dice, que cuando lo quiso hacer, asistiendo a ello la Santísima Trinidad, dijo: "Hagámosle a nuestra imagen y semejanza" ' (II, 206). Van Praag writes: '¿No es una tremenda burla que Guzmán, narrándonos la creación del hombre haga asistir a Dios en tal obra por la Santísima Trinidad?' This is because, in the mouth of a Jew, it can appear a sly dig against Christians to say that the Trinity created man, when there is no mention of the Trinity in *Genesis* or in the whole of the Old Testament. But, in fact, there is a change of phrasing in *Genesis*, I, 26. Whereas till then the words used had been 'Let there be light ... let there be a firmament,....', when it comes to the creation of man the Bible says: 'and God said, Let us make man in our image.' From the time of the earliest Fathers of the Church the use of the plural here was naturally taken as a reference to the

Trinity; while the works of the first five days were the creation of the Father, man was created by the three Persons because man was the crown of creation.[2] What van Praag takes to be a 'tremendous joke' is therefore a detail of traditional exegesis, so familiar that Calderón frequently repeats it when dramatizing the Creation in his *autos sacramentales*.[3]

[3] *Disregard of the context*. The following sentence is singled out as an irreverent joke on the Trinity: 'La Santísima Trinidad me lo dijo: ved a cuál de las tres personas queréis prender y castigar' (III, 95). In the context it is nothing of the sort, for these words are spoken by a simpleton – a weak-minded jester – in an anecdote illustrating the assertion that madmen and simpletons are often able unwittingly to speak home truths.

The following reference to a human monster is interpreted as mockery of the sign of the cross, since the latter is placed on the belly instead of on the forehead or chest: 'Tenía en el pecho figurado la Y pitagórica y en el estómago, hacia el vientre, una cruz bien formada' (I, 70). But this is a story of a monster born in Ravenna, whose deformities were a symbolic warning to the inhabitants of the calamities in store for them because of their wickedness: 'Pero la cruz y la Y eran señales buenas y dichosas, porque la Y en el pecho significaba virtud, y la cruz sobre el vientre, que si, reprimiendo las torpes carnalidades, abrazasen en su pecho la virtud, les daría Dios paz y ablandaría su ira' (I, 71). The symbolism is appropriate, the irreverent joke undetectable.

Van Praag alleges that saints are placed in a ridiculous light or are made fun of: for example 'Confía con que acá dejas capellanías y capilla de mi capa: que las misas no aprovechan a los condenados, aunque se las diga San Gregorio' (III, 266). The paragraph should be completed: 'No tienen ya remedio después de la sentencia'. The context is an attack on men who never make restitution of their ill-gotten goods in order to leave legacies for their children and for masses to be said for their souls; but if the testators go to hell, no masses will profit

them even if they are said by the greatest of saints – than
which nothing could be nearer the truth.

[4] *Failure to distinguish when Alemán speaks in character from
when he speaks in person.* There *is* a certain amount of irreverence and hypocrisy in the novel, but this is a phase of the delinquent's career, part of the evil of his life. Nobody has ever
claimed that Guzmán the *pícaro* was, as such, a devout moral-
ist: on the contrary, a sham religious edification was part of
the picaresque world. In *Rinconete y Cortadillo* the whole gang
of thieves go regularly to church and practise their devotions,
professing to think that they are thereby living honest lives.
Nobody has ever suggested that Cervantes is here ridiculing
the practice of going to church rather than the hypocrisy of
the scamps. Yet van Praag assumes that Alemán is mocking
Catholicism when he makes Guzmán say of himself: 'Ama-
neció el domingo. Púseme de ostentación y di de golpe con mi
lozanía en la iglesia mayor para oír misa; aunque sospecho que
más me llevó la gana de ser mirado; paseéla toda tres o cuatro
veces: visité las capillas donde acudía más gente, hasta que
vine a parar entre los dos coros, donde estaban muchas damas
y galanes' (II, 119). For Guzmán attendance at church was
a social entertainment – how could it not have been for one of
his manner of life? But why presume that it was so for
Alemán?

When Guzmán learns how to become a beggar in Rome he
is taught how to exploit hypocritically the piety of those who
give alms: 'Éste me enseñó a los principios cómo había de
pedir a los unos y a los otros; que no a todos ha de ser con un
tono ni con una arenga. Los hombres no quieren plagas, sino
una demanda llana, por amor de Dios; las mujeres tienen de-
voción a la Virgen María, a Nuestra Señora del Rosario. Y
así: "¡Dios encamine sus cosas en su santo servicio y las
libre de pecado mortal, de falso testimonio, de poder de
traidores y de malas lenguas!" Esto les arranca el dinero de
cuajo, bien pronunciado y con vehemencia de palabras reci-
tado' (II, 180-1). This is Guzmán deceitfully exploiting

religion, not Alemán mocking it. Time and time again van Praag attributes to the latter an irreverence that belongs to the former.

All the alleged examples of Alemán's ironical, mocking treatment of Christian doctrines and practices come under one or other of these four headings. No single one bears examination. There is therefore no evidence in the text for van Praag's contention that Alemán, being a Jew by descent, was not a sincere Christian.

NOTES

1. Vol. 11, 126. All references are to the Clásicos Castellanos edition.
2. e.g. 'Nunc tamen ut opera sex dierum nostra inquisitio pertractatioque concludat, hoc primum breviter dicimus, non indifferenter accipiendum quod in aliis operibus dicitur, *Dixit Deus, Fiat*; hic autem, *Dixit Deus, Faciamus hominem ad imaginem et similitudinem nostram*: ad insinuandam scilicet, ut ita dicam pluralitatem personarum propter Patrem et Filium et Spiritum sanctum', etc. (St Augustine, *De Genesi ad Litteram*, Lib. III, cap. xix.)
3. e.g. '*Poder*. Venid, pues, y al Hombre hagamos. / *Agua*. ¿Hagamos, en plural, dijo? / *Aire*. Sí. *Agua*. Pues ¿cómo, si con sólo / "hágase" todo se hizo, / "hágase" no dijo al Hombre? / *Fuego*. Ese es evidente indicio / que puso en él más cuidado / que en todo.' (*La vida es sueño*, in *Obras completas*, vol. III, ed. A. Valbuena Prat, Aguilar, Madrid 1952, 1392a.)

The Genesis of the Picaresque

1. Frank W. Chandler *Romances of Roguery: an Episode in the History of the Novel. In two Parts. Part I, The Picaresque Novel in Spain* (New York 1899); reprinted as No. 31 in the Burt Franklin Bibliography and Reference Series (New York 1961). *The Literature of Roguery*, 2 vols. (London, Boston, and New York 1907).

2. Dámaso Alonso is a distinguished exception: a book entitled *España y la novela* has been announced and is eagerly awaited. From what is probably a foretaste of this ('The Spanish Contribution to the Modern European Novel', in *Journal of World History* VI, 1961, 878–97) it would seem that his study of novelistic realism will primarily cover characterization in a way that will exclude what for me is the special interest of the picaresque novel proper, as I develop it in these pages.

3. Harvard Studies in Comparative Literature, 26 (Cambridge, Massachusetts 1964).

4. By Elbert Lenrow (New York and London 1940).

5. Walter Allen *The English Novel* (Penguin Books 1958) 32.

6. F. McCombie '*Count Fathom* and *El Buscón*', in *Notes and Queries* New Series VII (1960) 297.

7. *Encyclopaedia Americana* (1959).

8. Op. cit., 68. This is symptomatic of a common tendency to see the Spanish literary *pícaro* as a type character with unchanging qualities exemplified by all. There is, in fact, no single type; instead of conventional uniformity there is great variation of characterization, tone, and aim in the novels. All generalizations that imply the contrary are misleading. Particularly dangerous are those that extract a universal 'picaresque philosophy' which all the novels illustrate. Rafael Benítez Claros, for

instance, sees the novels as foreshadowing Kierkegaardian problems and Sartre's existentialism (*Existencialismo y picaresca*, Colección 'O crece o muere' Madrid 1958). Domingo Pérez Minik says: 'We see the picaresque novel as life crucified on the pure absurd' ('Sentido vigente de la novela picaresca', in *Novelistas españoles de los siglos XIX y XX* Madrid 1957, 16.) All such generalizations are accompanied by a total absence of any literary analysis, of any desire to see or interpret any novel as a unit by itself.

9. This is interestingly portrayed in an engraved frontispiece to *La pícara Justina* (1605). While Celestina, Guzmán, and Justina are sailing in 'the ship of the picaresque life', Lázaro is not with them, but in a boat by himself. See frontispiece to this book.

10. 'PÍCARO. Bajo, ruin, doloso, falto de honra y vergüenza' (*Diccionario de Autoridades*). In modern Spanish the word, like our 'rascal', is undergoing a semantic change, since it can now be used as a term of endearment.

11. Mary Morse *The Unattached* (Pelican Books 1965) 75–6.

12. 'The Image of the Delinquent in Literature, 1955–1960', in *Metaphor and Symbol* ed. L. C. Knights and Basil Cottle, Proceedings of the Twelfth Symposium of the Colston Research Society held in the University of Bristol (London 1960) 28.

13. Marcel Bataillon has maintained that the history of literature would be clarified if *Lazarillo* were no longer considered the first picaresque novel: Introduction to *La Vie de Lazarillo de Tormès* (Collection Bilingue des Classiques Espagnols, Paris 1958) 75 ff. Alberto del Monte considers *Lazarillo* the 'archetype' of the *genre* but *Guzmán de Alfarache* as its first 'document': *Itinerario del Romanzo Picaresco Spagnolo* (Florence 1957) 44. Gonzalo Sobejano insists that *Lazarillo* is the 'first stage' of the *genre* and that *Guzmán* derives from it ('De la intención y valor del "Guzmán de Alfarache" ', in *Romanische Forschungen* LXXI [1959] 266–311), but the reasons he gives are precisely those that make me call it the 'precursor'.

14. Lionel Stevenson *The English Novel, a Panorama* (London 1960) 31–2.

15. This is the burden of del Monte's study, op. cit., which is one

of the better modern treatments of the subject. It has been emphatically driven home in a more recent study: O. Borgers, 'Le Roman picaresque. Réalisme et fiction', in *Lettres Romanes* XIV (1960) 295–305; XV (1961) 23–38, 135–48.

16. C. J. Ribton-Turner *A History of Vagrants and Vagrancy and Beggars and Begging* (London 1887) 100–62, 517–65. There has been no modern history of this subject to supersede this standard work.

17. Ribton-Turner, op. cit., 519–22. He gives no sources for his account of France, but it agrees with the rather fuller account in Maxime du Camp, *Paris, ses organes, ses fonctions et sa vie dans la seconde moitié du XIXe siècle* (5th ed., Paris 1875) IV, 5–15. Du Camp gives as his source: Henri Sauval, *Histoire et recherches des antiquités de la ville de Paris* (Paris 1724) 3 vols.; I have not seen this work.

18. This was edited by Luther in 1528 with the title *Von der falschen Bettler Büberei*. English translation by J. C. Hotten, *The Book of Vagabonds* (1860).

19. *Il vagabondo ovvero sferza de' Bianti e Vagabondi* (Venice 1627), published under the pseudonym of Rafaele Frianoro.

20. *The Elizabethan Underworld. A Collection of Tudor and early Stuart Tracts and Ballads telling of the Lives and Misdoings of Vagabonds, Thieves, Rogues and Cozeners...* The Text prepared with Notes and an Introduction by A. V. Judges (London 1930) xv.

21. W. P. M. Kennedy, *Parish Life under Elizabeth*, 149–51 (quoted by A. V. Judges, *The Elizabethan Underworld*, liii).

22. This Order, drawn up on 16 September 1603 by the Chief Justice and Attorney General, is interesting enough to be quoted in full: 'Forasmuch as it hath appeared unto us as well by our own views in our travels in this present progress of his Majesty as also by good and credible information from diverse and sundry parts of the realm that rogues grow again to increase and be incorrigible and dangerous, not only to his Majesty's loving subjects abroad, but also to his Majesty and his most honourable Household and attendants in and about his Court, which growing partly through the remissness of some Justices of the Peace and other officers of the country, and partly for that there hath been no suit made for assigning

some place beyond the seas to which such incorrigible or dangerous rogues might be banished according to the statute in that behalf made [a reference to 39 Eliz. c. 4 (1597–8)]; we therefore of his Majesty's Privy Council whose names are hereunto subscribed, finding it of necessity to reform great abuses and to have the due execution of so good and necessary a law, do according to the power limited unto us by the same statute hereby assign and think it fit and expedient that the places and parts beyond the seas to which any such incorrigible or dangerous rogues shall be banished and conveyed according to the said statute shall be these countries and places following, viz. the New Found Land, the East or West Indies, France, Germany, Spain and the Low Countries or any of them' (*Acts of the Privy Council of England* New Series XXXII, 503–4).

23. E.g. Rafael Salillas, *El delincuente español. Hampa*. (*Antropología picaresca*) (Madrid 1898) 50; and Manuel de Montolíu, *El alma de España y sus reflejos en la literatura del siglo de oro* (Barcelona [1942]) 265.

24. 'Perspectiva de la novela picaresca', in *Hacia Cervantes* (2nd. ed., Madrid 1960); this essay, originally published in 1935, is here expanded.

25. *The Structure of Spanish History* (Princeton 1954) 564–70, 557, n. 16; 'Perspectiva de la novela picaresca', ed. cit., *passim*. See also 'El "Lazarillo de Tormes" ', in *Hacia Cervantes* (2nd ed.) 135–41.

26. It has been too readily assumed from the existence of obscure periods in Mateo Alemán's life that he was a social failure and misfit. New documents, which Professor Germán Bleiberg of Vanderbilt University has discovered and is publishing, show that his standing in the government service was high and that he was at one time appointed the official commissioner to investigate and report on charges that the criminals sentenced to work in the mines of Almadén were being ill-treated.

27. M. Bataillon 'Les Nouveaux chrétiens dans l'essor du roman picaresque', in *Neophilologus* XLVIII (1964) 283–98: and the summary of his course of lectures in *l'Annuaire du Collège de France* (1963) 485–90.

28. *Exemplary Novels*, trans. N. Maccoll (Glasgow 1902) II, 34. ('Trece años, o poco más, tendría Carriazo, cuando, llevado de

una inclinación picaresca, sin forzarle a ello algún mal trata-
miento que sus padres le hiciesen, sólo por su gusto y antojo
se desgarró, como dicen los muchachos, de casa de sus padres,
y se fue por ese mundo adelante, tan contento de la vida
libre, que, en la mitad de las incomodidades y miserias que
trae consigo, no echaba menos la abundancia de la casa de su
padre, ni el andar a pie le cansaba, ni el frío le ofendía, ni el
calor le enfadaba. Para él todos los tiempos del año le eran
dulce y templada primavera. Tan bien dormía en parvas, como
en colchones; con tanto gusto se soterraba en un pajar de un
mesón, como si se acostara entre dos sábanas de holanda.
Finalmente, él salió tan bien con el asunto de pícaro, que
pudiera leer cátedra en la facultad al famoso de Alfarache.'
Novelas Ejemplares, ed. R. Schevill and A. Bonilla, Madrid
1923, II, 267–8.)

29. Ibid., 35. ('...allí van o envían muchos padres principales a
buscar a sus hijos, y los hallan: y tanto sienten sacarlos de
aquella vida, como si los llevaran a dar la muerte', ibid., 269.)

30. Agustín González de Amezúa *Cervantes, creador de la novela
corta española* (Madrid 1958) 295–6.

31. Part I, Bk. ii, cap. 2.

32. 'Gozar de libertad, vivir contento,/soñarse Rey vistiéndose de
andrajos,/comer faisanes siendo solos ajos/y poseer alegre
el pensamiento' (ed. A. Bonilla y San Martín, *Anales de la
literatura española*, Madrid 1904, 64–75). This interlude was
originally published (Alcalá 1614) under the pseudonym
Damón de Henares; Bonilla identified the author as Pedro
Láinez (d. 1605).

33. 'Muy largo procedía y corto quedo/en alabar la vida que
codicio/.../sólo el pícaro muere bien logrado,/que desde
que nació, nada desea,/y así lo tiene todo acaudalado./.../sus
alcázares altos son los suelos,/estables cuanto el mundo
mundo fuere,/y tesoreros ricos de los cielos' (ed. A. Bonilla
y San Martín *Revue Hispanique* IX, 1902, 295–330). The
Catálogo of Salvá lists an anonymous edition of 1601 which
nobody has since seen. The poem is attributed in MSS to
Pedro Liñán de Riaza and to Lupercio Leonardo de Argensola.

34. First suggested by Manuel de Montolíu (op. cit., 274–5), this
thesis has been developed by J. Frutos Gómez de las Cortinas,

'El antihéroe y su actitud vital (sentido de la novela picaresca)',
in *Cuadernos de literatura* VII (1950) 97–145.

35. 'Vestís a vuestro gusto, coméis de vuestra mano, nadie os la
besa para engañaros...No tenéis pretensiones, pleitos no os
desvelan...si se os mancha el vestido no se os mancha el
honor. Vivís con excepción de leyes de cortesía...y, al fin, sois
príncipes de vuestra voluntad, ejecutores de vuestras rentas...
Sois república exenta, pueblo sin guerras, y en todo señoría
libre...Dios os guarde de ser caballeros' (Félix Machado de
Silva, Marqués de Montebelo, *Tercera parte de Guzmán de
Alfarache*; ed. Gerhard Moldenhauer, *Revue Hispanique* LXIX
[1927] 1–340). The work was to have been published under
the name Félix Marqués.

36. *Erasme et l'Espagne. Recherches sur l'histoire spirituelle du
XVIᵉ siècle* (Paris 1937). For the literary theories of the early
humanists see pp. 651–62.

37. For an account of this literature, which Bataillon calls 'une
littérature de vérité', see ibid., 663–735. Among these Erasmian
writings there is a Latin dialogue, *Eremitae* (1538?), by Juan
Maldonado in which some hermits recount to each other their
lives in the world. One of these lives, that of Gonzalo, is
described by Bataillon as 'un assez beau scénario de roman,
d'un roman picaresque qui annonce *Guzman de Alfarache* plus
que *Lazarille*' (p. 690).

38. *La vida de Lazarillo de Tormes: y de sus fortunas y adversidades*
(Burgos 1554); there were two other editions the same year
at Alcalá de Henares and Antwerp. The first English translation, by David Rowland, was published in 1586 (though
there may have been an earlier edition, now lost, in 1576).

39. *Introducción del símbolo de la fe* (Salamanca 1582); ed. Biblioteca de Autores Españoles VI, 327b. Granada is contrasting the
pleasure derived from reading of fictitious heroisms with the
much greater, and more profitable, pleasure that would be
derived from reading of the bravery of true heroes, like the
Christian martyrs.

40. *Libro de la conversión de la Magdalena, en que se exponen los tres
estados que tuvo de pecadora, y de penitente, y de gracia* (Barcelona 1588). There is a modern edition in Clásicos Castellanos.

41. *Primera Parte de Guzmán de Alfarache* (Madrid 1599).

42. The relation of *Lazarillo* to *Guzmán* and the picaresque *genre* is beautifully indicated in the frontispiece to *La pícara Justina*: while Lázaro is outside the 'ship of the picaresque life', his little boat is towing it. See frontispiece to this book.

43. Part II, Bk. iii, cap. 3 (ed. Clásicos Castellanos, IV 249–51).

44. *Segunda Parte de la vida de Guzmán de Alfarache, atalaya de la vida humana, por Mateo Alemán, su verdadero autor* (Lisbon 1604). Martí published his apocryphal continuation under a pseudonym: *Segunda Parte de la vida del pícaro Guzmán de Alfarache. Compuesto por Mateo Luján de Sayavedra* (Valencia 1602).

45. They are *El crótalon* (ed. Nueva Biblioteca de Autores Españoles, VII) and *Viaje de Turquía* (ibid., 11). Both are anonymous and both have been attributed with insufficient foundation to Cristóbal de Villalón and reprinted under his name in the Colección Austral. Marcel Bataillon has identified the author of the *Viaje* as Andrés Laguna (*Le Docteur Laguna auteur du Voyage en Turquie*, Paris 1958). For both works see his *Érasme en Espagne*, 698–735.

46. *Érasme en Espagne*, 652–3.

47. 'La intención religiosa del *Lazarillo de Tormes* y Juan de Valdés', in *Hispanic Review* XXVII (1959) 78–102. Though the actual attribution to Valdés is rash, the novel is placed very convincingly into an Erasmian *milieu*. Arguments are also adduced in favour of an early date of composition, *c.* 1525.

48. F. McCombie, 'Count Fathom and El Buscón', loc. cit.; Fernando Lázaro Carreter, 'Originalidad del Buscón', in *Studia Philologica, Homenaje ofrecido a Dámaso Alonso* (Madrid 1961) II, 319–38.

49. E. A. Baker *The History of the English Novel* (London 1929) III, 190–1.

50. See E. C. Riley *Cervantes's Theory of the Novel* (Oxford 1962) 155–6.

51. Erich Auerbach *Mimesis: dargestellte Wirklichkeit in der abendländischen Literatur* (Berne 1946); Engl. trans. *Mimesis: the Representation of Reality in Western Literature* (Princeton 1953, and Anchor Books, New York 1957).

52. Cap. 2 and *passim*. The criticism of Spanish literature in general comes at the end of cap. 13, that of Cervantes in cap. 14.

53. This chapter will have made clear that I use 'realism' to denote primarily a technique ('fidelity of representation' as against 'idealism') and secondarily an attitude in the writer to his subject-matter and to his readers ('truthfulness' and 'responsibility' as against 'escapism'). I do not wish to imply at any time that the 'realism' of picaresque novels, in both senses, is either uniform or constant. Carlos Blanco Aguinaga argues, in an interesting paper, that it is misleading and confusing to include Cervantes with the picaresque novelists under the single term 'realism', for they exemplify two opposing ways of conceiving a novel–'dogmatic realism' and 'objective realism' ('Cervantes y la picaresca. Notas sobre dos tipos de realismo', in *Nueva Revista de Filología Hispánica* XI, 1957, 313–42). For me there can be as many varieties of 'realism' as there are writers employing the technique, and it is as misleading to postulate a single ('dogmatic') realism for all Spanish picaresque novelists as it would be to assume (what no one has ever done) that Alemán and Cervantes are similar in technique, tone and attitude of mind because they are both realistic writers.

After this book was completed I received from the author, Don Lorenzo Polaino Ortega, a copy of his *La delincuencia en la picaresca* (Seville 1964), which is a short preliminary study of the aspects of criminal law portrayed in the Spanish novels.

2

The Delinquent Emerges

1. I do not use 'social interest' in Auerbach's rather restrictive sense: I mean an interest in the ways in which the different relations between men, as determined by the hierarchical structure of society, affect their values and conduct in practice. For excellent analyses of *Lazarillo* from rather different standpoints, see the Introductions to the editions of Marcel Bataillon (Collection Bilingue des Classiques Espagnols, Paris 1958) and R.O. Jones (Manchester University Press 1963).

2. *Lección y sentido del Guzmán de Alfarache* (Revista de Filología Española, Anejo XL, Madrid 1948).

3. *Itinerario del romanzo picaresco spagnolo* (Florence 1957) 65, n. 1.

4. 'Sobre el sentido del Guzmán de Alfarache', in *Estudios dedicados a Menéndez Pidal*, V (1954) 283-306.

5. *S. Antonio de Padua. De Mateo Alemán* (Lisbon 1605). The two *aprobaciones* are dated 24 November and 7 December, 1603; the work was therefore written before Part II of *Guzmán* was published; although the forthcoming publication of the latter is announced here in the preliminaries, it actually appeared first.

6. 'Y así, después que ha visto/vuestra fe, religión, pluma y deseo,/os hace el nuevo Cristo/que ha transformado amor, nuevo Mateo;/del mundo os alza el vuelo:/él vuela en vuestra pluma, y vos al Cielo.' Van Praag had not seen this work when he wrote his article. It is so full of legendary miracles that a modern reader might well be tempted to see it as an ironical exposure of the superstitious aspects of the Catholicism of the times; but in this respect it is in no way

different from, for instance, the *Flos sanctorum* (1599–1601) of the Jesuit Ribadeneira. Alemán's taste in hagiography is that of his age; it is certainly not our taste.

7. The interesting suggestion that the picaresque novel owed its origin to the influence of sermons was put forward by Miguel Herrero 'Nueva interpretación de la novela picaresca', in *Revista de Filología Española*, XXIV (1937) 343–62. It was based on the didactic and ascetic character of *Guzmán*, and on the fact that sermons were divided into two parts, a theoretical exposition and a practical illustration from real life. According to Herrero, the picaresque novels could have been expansions of the sort of illustrations given in the second part of sermons. The weakness of this thesis is that no supporting examples are given, and though Herrero later studied the sermons of the period, he never followed up this idea. It is, I think, more helpful in explaining the structure of *Guzmán* than its plot.

8. Op. cit., 167.

9. '...porque como sean las vidas de santos ejemplos a las nuestras, tengo por permitido a un claro y fiel espejo cristalino de roca, donde nos habemos de mirar, ponerle algunos adornos con que se guarnezca; y a semejantes lecturas irlas parafraseando con moralidades y alegorías de donde se saque fruto, cual confío en la divina majestad lo hará en ésta.' (Prologue.)

10. 'Costumbre mía es, y no la tengo por mala, ir en mis escritos llevando por delante la parte curiosa de aquello que se me ofrece, por no hacer otro camino' (fol. 12v.). 'Y si todavía no te parecieren de este lugar, yo se lo tengo de dar: porque lo bueno, en toda parte lo tiene' (fol. 14r).

11. This explanation has a touch of disingenuousness about it, and those who stress the importance of Alemán's Jewish ancestry have here missed a clear enough example of his consciousness of it. By this long opening digression, he honours not only St Anthony but himself, for among the heroes of Portuguese history is a Don Enrique Alemán who was killed in the crusade against the Moors, who was venerated as a saint and whose tomb was the scene of some miracles. Alemán does not claim him as an ancestor, but the reader is of course made to associate his surname with Catholic orthodoxy in its highest and most heroic form.

12. For examples see Moreno Báez, op. cit., 79–84.
13. Since it is often stated or implied that these defects exist
    because the novel was produced in the Spain of that period
    and not in a freer air, it should be pointed out that none of
    this criticism was apparent to Ben Jonson or to James Mabbe
    when the latter published his English translation of *Guzmán*
    in 1622. In his dedication (written in Spanish) to Sir John
    Strangwayes, Mabbe emphasizes that the Spanish picaroon is
    no idle talker but earnest and morally instructive, as well as
    witty, and that nothing would be further from the truth than
    the allegation that the work is ill-digested and disorderly.
    Ben Jonson, in a poem introducing and praising the translation,
    writes: '...this Spanish Proteus; who, though writ / But
    in one tongue, was formed with the world's wit: / And hath the
    noblest mark of a Good Book, / That an ill man dares not
    securely look / Upon it, but will loath or let it pass, / As a
    deformèd face doth a true glass' (*The Rogue, or the Life of
    Guzman de Alfarache...done into English by James Mabbe*,
    Tudor Translations, Second Series, London 1924, 1, 5–6, 31).
14. Addressing the reader: 'aquesta confesión general que hago,
    este alarde público que de mis cosas lo represento' (Part 11,
    Bk. i, cap. 1). An ordinary confession covers the period since
    the penitent's last confession, a general confession covers the
    penitent's whole life.
15. This is the seventh class of Italian beggar listed by Giacinto
    Nobili in 1627, that of the '*Accaponi*, or Ulcerated, who made
    ulcers on their legs with powder, toast, and hare's blood'
    (C. J. Ribton-Turner *A History of Vagrants and Vagrancy*,
    London 1887, 558).
16. Moreno Báez (op. cit., 51–2) believes that Alemán never
    intended to write a Third Part, since in his preface to Part I
    he stated that Guzmán 'writes his life in the galleys' which is
    where he leaves him at the end of Part 11, and since the re-
    pentance he there undergoes is the logical end to the work.
    For me, on the other hand, Alemán's later reference to the
    continuation in Part 11 is conclusive: 'Servirán aquí mis penas
    para excusarte de ellas, informándote para que sepas
    encadenar lo pasado y presente con lo venidero de la tercera
    parte y que, hecho de todo un trabado contexto, quedes cual

debes, instruido en las veras' (Part II, Bk. i, cap. 1).
[In Mabbe's translation: 'For my punishments and my misfortunes, if thou wilt truly inform thyself of them, will serve
thee instead of a looking-glass, whereby thou mayest see how
to link a little better together the past and the present with
that which is to come in the Third Part; to the end that, thou
making it all one continued piece of work, wearing it well and
handsomely, running along in even threads, thou mayest the
better (which is no more than becomes thee) be instructed in
the truth of things']. The connected unity of doctrinal truth
which Alemán here stresses necessitates, as an indispensable
logical conclusion, the life of penitence and grace to follow
repentance for the life of sin. That the present ending is not
felt to be logical is shown by the fact that so many critics
reject Guzmán's conversion as 'inorganic', i.e. not part of a
'trabado contexto'. The form the Third Part would probably
have taken is discussed in Chapter IV.

17. Mabbe's translation (ed. cit., I, 62), in which I have corrected
his rendering 'when the whole current ran', *cuando* here being
synonymous with *como sea que*. ('Ves aquí...que cuando todo
corra turbio, iba mi padre con el hilo de la gente y no fue sólo
el que pecó...Ténganos Dios de su mano para no caer en
otras o semejantes miserias, que todos somos hombres.'
Part I, Bk. i, cap. 1). Carlos Blanco Aguinaga (op. cit.,
316–19) has seen the opening of *Guzmán* as clearly symbol-
izing original sin, but on the basis only of the furtive love-
making from which the protagonist was born; he also draws
some conclusions from this that seem to me erroneous:
'Desde el principio de la novela estamos, pues, en el símbolo
del dogma del pecado original, fruto del libre albedrío, que
pesa sobre la vida toda y la determina a más libre albedrío y,
por alguna razón inescrutable, a más pecado.' He seems to
consider original sin to be some force that 'determines'
human free-will to further sin; not unnaturally he finds this
'paradoxical'. As a result of this determination, 'no logra
Guzmán librarse ni de la mancha de su herencia ni de las
circunstancias que, creadas a su vez, por la misma herencia,
lo van empujando más y más a vivir en el pecado del mundo'
(319). There is no sign in the novel of heredity creating

circumstances that determine to sin and that create other circumstances that determine to further sin; there are only perfectly plausible reactions of a given human temperament to a succession of environmental influences. There is nothing either deterministic or paradoxical about the Christian (or at least the Catholic) dogma of original sin; it is a mystery (and therefore a dogma) only as regards the way in which guilt and its effects are *transmitted* through the whole human race; there is nothing mysterious about the effects themselves, for earthly paradises and golden ages have never been more than dreams and all men, at all times, have always known that human children do not grow up with a *natural* inclination to innocence and virtue and a *natural* control of their passions. Guzmán's entry into the world is placed in the setting of human experience and so is the whole of his progress to the galleys; what Alemán adds to this by way of 'symbolism' and commentary is a theological framework that offers an interpretation of that experience in its totality.

18. 'The shame that I had to return home, I lost it upon the way; for travelling afoot as I did, it weighed so heavy, that I was not able to bring it along with me: or perhaps, they that stole my cloak, carried it away with them in the cape thereof; and this is sure the likelier of the two. For ever since that time I have been troubled with a lazy kind of yawning, and a fever-lordane, which did prognosticate the disease [I should be sick of to my dying day]. A pox upon shamefastness, which hung still upon me, and yet I had none of it; for I began to free myself from that irksomeness, and that little shame that was left me, I turned into impudency: for hunger and shame could never yet be made friends.' (Ed. cit., I, 251.) ('La vergüenza que tuve de volverme perdíla por los caminos: que como vine a pie y pesaba tanto, no pude traerla o quizá me la llevaron en la capilla de la capa. Y así debió de ser, pues desde entonces tuve unos bostezos y calosfríos que pronosticaron mi enfermedad. Maldita sea la vergüenza que me quedó ni ya tenía, porque me comencé a desenfadar y lo que tuve de vergonzoso lo hice desenvoltura: que nunca pudieron ser amigos la hambre y la vergüenza.' Part I, Bk. ii, cap. 2).

19. See Part I, Bk. iii, cap. 2–3.

20. Mabbe, IV, 327–8. ('De donde vine a considerar y díjeme una
noche a mí mismo: ¿Ves aquí, Guzmán, la cumbre del monte
de las miserias, adonde te ha subido tu torpe sensualidad?
Ya estás arriba o para dar un salto en lo profundo de los
infiernos o para con facilidad, alzando el brazo, alcanzar el
cielo.' Part II, Bk. iii, cap. 8).

21. An analysis of the character of Guzmán very different from the
above is given by Sherman Eoff ('The Picaresque Psychology
of Guzmán de Alfarache', in *Hispanic Review*, XXI [1953]
107–19). Eoff presents this as agreeing substantially with the
analysis of the *pícaro*'s character in *El buscón* which I had
published in 1947 (and which I reproduce in the following
chapter). To have applied the same approach to Guzmán was
misguided, for Alemán's standpoint and aim are quite
different from those of Quevedo. The former presents delinquency as a conflict between reason and will in terms of
traditional moral theology (like the conflicts between *El
Entendimiento* and *El Albedrío* in the *autos sacramentales* of
Calderón), and did not intuit along modern lines a relationship
between character and environment, much less compensation
for an inferiority complex, as Quevedo did. Eoff's analysis
and conclusion are invalidated not only by this wrong approach
but also by his failure to distinguish between Guzmán *qua*
agent and *qua* narrator (as when he states that Guzmán
'attacks the "vanas honras" of the wealthy and privileged
groups whose ranks he constantly strives to join', 115).
Guzmán is thus presented as 'one who is a failure and who
tries desperately to convince himself that he is a success'
(118). Since 'success' here means only material prosperity
and social standing, the conversion is misunderstood, being
cheapened into 'an expression of a desire to be in an approved
social position' (114). The whole point of the novel, and its
profundity, lies in the fact that real success comes only when,
and because, Guzmán climbs up to 'the top of the mountain
of miseries'.

22. Mabbe, IV, 346. I have modified the last sentence where
Mabbe's rendering fails to convey the correct nuance: 'as that
all of them did verily believe, that I did justly deserve this
punishment, and therefore took no pity of me.' ('Y el mayor

dolor que sentí en aquel desastre, no tanto era el dolor que padecia ni ver el falso testimonio que se me levantaba, sino que juzgasen todos que de aquel castigo era merecedor y no se dolían de mí.' Part II, Bk. iii, cap. 9).

23. Recent examples are: Francisco Maldonado de Guevara (see p. 170 below); S. Eoff, who sees it as 'an obvious manipulation on the part of the author to illustrate and terminate a moral theme' (op. cit., 114); Alberto del Monte, who sees it as out of harmony with the tone of the work (op. cit., 73–4). G. Sobejano, op. cit., does not query the conversion, but he does seek to minimize the religious intention of the book in order to safeguard its satirico-didactic purpose – as if the one denied the other.

24. *Libro de entretenimiento de la pícara Justina, en el cual debajo de graciosos discursos se encierran provechosos avisos* (Medina del Campo 1605). The licence to print is dated August 22, 1604. The book finishes with Justina's first marriage and with the statement that the Second Part will include her third marriage, to Guzmán de Alfarache, whose wife she is at the time of writing but could scarcely have claimed to be had Alemán's Second Part already appeared.

25. 'El Quijote de Avellaneda', reprinted in *Estudios y discursos de crítica histórica y literaria* (Edición Nacional, Madrid 1941) I, 377.

26. Bataillon is preparing an annotated edition of *La pícara Justina*. The following comprises what he has so far published by way of a general interpretation of the novel, analyses of particular sections and studies of the problem of authorship: 'Urganda entre *Don Quixote* et *La pícara Justina*', in *Studia Philologica: Homenaje ofrecido a Dámaso Alonso* (Madrid 1960) I, 191–215; 'Une vision burlesque des monuments de León en 1602', in *Bulletin Hispanique*, LXIII (1961) 169–78; 'Ríoseco? La "morería" de La Pícara Justina', in *Études d'Orientalisme dédiées à la mémoire de Lévi-Provençal* (Paris 1962) 13–21; ' "La picaresca". À propos de *La pícara Justina*', in *Wort und Text. Festschrift für Fritz Schalk* (Frankfurt am Main 1963) 233–50; 'Style, genre et sens. Les asturiens de *La pícara Justina*', in *Linguistic and Literary Studies in Honor of Helmut A. Hatzfeld* (Washington, D.C., 1964) 47–59; and in

the following issues of *l'Annuaire du Collège de France* (1959) 567–9 (1960) 416–20 (1961) 399–404.

27. He makes 'the author of *La pícara Justina*' one of the leaders of the army of pseudo-poets invading Parnassus; he causes havoc by the *librazo* ('hefty book') he hurls at Apollo's camp (*Viaje al Parnaso*, ed. R. Schevill and A. Bonilla, Madrid 1922, 100). He attacks *haldeando* ('with his skirts flying'), a phrase that can apply not only to a cassock but to a physician's gown; and the term *capellán lego*, which Cervantes applies to him means, not an 'ignorant' chaplain, but a 'lay' one, i.e. a layman holding a position of confidential adviser similar to that of a chaplain; Bataillon considers that he must also have had something of the function of a jester in one or more noble families.

28. 'Fertur apud nos auctor esse et illius libelli, quem Francisco Ubedae Toletano typi adjudicant, *La pícara Justina* nuncupatum, cum liceret sic per aetatem insanire' (*Bibliotheca Hispana Nova*, 1672, entry under F. Andreas Pérez). This reference to the age of Fr. Pérez has been taken to mean his dotage. It never occurred to Puyol y Alonso, who argued in favour of his authorship, that it could be construed in any other sense, although he was unable to explain how a friar who published his first book in 1601, who became a master of novices in that year after having been a professor in the Dominican College at Valladolid, and who was to publish volumes of sermons in 1621 and 1622, could be in his dotage in 1604 when he could scarcely have been older than 54 (*La pícara Justina*, ed. Julio Puyol y Alonso, Sociedad de Bibliófilos Madrileños, Madrid 1912, III, 46–93). Obviously, Antonio's phrase can only mean that it would not have been lawful for Fr. Pérez to write a foolish burlesque book after he had become a professed religious, *per aetatem* meaning 'because of his youth'.

29. 'My design has been to place in the market-place of our commonwealth a [billiard] table at which everyone can succeed in entertaining himself without fear of injury, I mean without hurt to mind or body because virtuous and agreeable exercises rather benefit than harm. It is so, for people are not always at church, the oratories are not always occupied, men

are not always taken up with affairs, however [worthy these may be]. There are hours of recreation when the harassed spirit may rest. For this purpose avenues are planted, fountains are sought for, slopes are levelled, and gardens are cultivated with care' (*Exemplary Novels*, trans. N. Maccoll [Glasgow 1902] I, 6). ('Mi intento ha sido poner en la plaza de nuestra república una mesa de trucos, donde cada uno pueda llegar a entretenerse, sin daño de barras; digo sin daño del alma ni del cuerpo, porque los ejercicios honestos y agradables, antes aprovechan que dañan. Sí, que no siempre se está en los templos; no siempre se ocupan los oratorios; no siempre se asiste a los negocios, por calificados que sean. Horas hay de recreación, donde el afligido espíritu descanse. Para este efecto se plantan las alamedas, se buscan las fuentes, se allanan las cuestas y se cultivan, con curiosidad, los jardines.')

30. 'Es tan sutil el engaño y engaños de la carne, que a los broncos, zafios e ignorantes, persuade sus embustes y embeleca con sus regalos' (Bk. II, Part i, cap. 1; *La novela picaresca española*, ed. Angel Valbuena Prat, 4th ed. Madrid 1962, 753–4).

Zenith and Nadir in Spain

1. *Relaciones de la vida del escudero Marcos de Obregón* (Madrid 1618).
2. George Haley *Vicente Espinel and Marcos de Obregón: A Life and its Literary Representation* Brown University Series XXV (Providence, Rhode Island 1959).
3. 'El intento mío fue ver si acertaría a escribir en prosa algo que aprovechase a mi república, deleitando y enseñando, siguiendo aquel consejo de mi maestro Horacio; porque han salido algunos libros de hombres doctísimos en letras y opinión que se abrazan tanto con sola la doctrina, que no dejan lugar donde pueda el ingenio alentarse y recibir gusto; y otros tan enfrascados en parecerles que deleitan con burlas y cuentos entremesiles, que después de haberlos revuelto, ahechado y aun cernido, son tan fútiles y vanos que no dejan cosa de sustancia ni provecho para el lector, ni de fama y opinión para sus autores.'
4. A Madrid edition of 1804 changes the title to *El donado hablador, vida y aventura de Alonso*, etc.; the novel is now commonly called by this title, which means 'The Talkative Lay-brother'.
5. *Historia de la vida del buscón, llamado don Pablos, ejemplo de vagamundos y espejo de tacaños* (Saragossa 1626). It has been alleged by Felicidad Buendía that the Inquisition 'persecuted' *El buscón* after Quevedo's death, since she publishes a document of 1646 in which an official of the Inquisition reports that the novel is on sale at a bookshop, despite the fact that the latest Index has prohibited all Quevedo's works except those he has acknowledged to be his, which do not include this novel. (Quevedo *Obras completas*, II, *Obras en verso*, Aguilar,

Madrid 1960, 1103–4). While it is possible that Quevedo may have found difficulty in publishing *El buscón* as he did his *Sueños*, because some of his jokes were on the border-line of irreverence, once it was published the Inquisition never interfered with any of its numerous editions, either during Quevedo's lifetime or after his death. The only probable explanation of this document is the following. We know that on his release from captivity in 1643, Quevedo began to prepare an edition of his Collected Works, for which he obtained a licence in 1644. Since he had been often attacked for the alleged malice and virulence of his satires, he would now have been anxious, knowing himself to be near to death, to exclude any such works from his projected edition. He therefore 'repudiated' *El buscón*; but since he died in the following year, his repudiation had no effect.

6. In 1657 (from the French), 1707 (by John Stevens in *The Comical Works of Don Francisco de Quevedo*) and three modern ones: by Charles Duff *The Life of the Great Rascal*, included in the volume of Quevedo's *Choice Humorous and Satirical Works* in the Broadway Translations (London and New York 1926); by Frank Mugglestone (under the pseudonym Francisco Villamiquel y Hardin), *The Life and Adventures of Don Pablos the Sharper* (The Anglo-Spanish Library, Leicester 1928); and by Hugh A. Harter, *The Scavenger* (Las Americas Publishing Co., New York 1962).

7. Harter, op. cit., 32.

8. 'Trajeron exploradores que nos buscasen los ojos por toda la cara; y a mí, como había sido mi trabajo mayor y la hambre imperial–que al fin me trataban como a criado–en buen rato no me los hallaron. Trajeron médicos, y mandaron que nos limpiasen con zorras el polvo de las bocas, como retablos, y bien lo éramos de duelos…Mandaron los doctores que por nueve días no hablase nadie recio en nuestro aposento, porque como estaban huecos los estómagos, sonaba en ellos el eco de cualquier palabra. Con estas y otras prevenciones comenzamos a volver y cobrar algún aliento; pero nunca podían las quijadas desdoblarse, que estaban magras y alforzadas, y así se dió orden que cada día nos las ahormasen con la mano del almirez.' (Cap. IV, pp. 46–8. All references are to the edition

by Américo Castro in Clásicos Castellanos; the current edition, 1960, has several printing errors which I have corrected from the first edition of 1927 in the passages I quote. The critical edition of Fernando Lázaro Carreter, *La vida del buscón, llamado don Pablos*, in Clásicos Hispánicos, Salamanca 1965, did not come to my notice until after the completion of this book.)

9. 'La sotana era milagrosa, porque no se sabía de qué color era. Unos, viéndola tan sin pelo, la tenían por de cuero de rana; otros decían que era ilusión; desde cerca parecía negra, y desde lejos entre azul; traíala sin ciñidor. No traía cuellos ni puños; parecía, con los cabellos largos y la sotana mísera, lacayuelo de la muerte. Cada zapato podía ser tumba de un filisteo' (Cap. III; 34).

10. The joke is introduced through a pun on *real*: 'costáronme veinte o treinta reales, y eran más para ver que cuantos tiene el rey, pues por éstos se veía de puros rotos, y por esotros no se verá nada' (Cap. XXII; 245).

11. 'Dicen que era de muy buena cepa; y, según él bebió, puédese muy bien creer' (p. 16). 'Murió el angelito de unos azotes que le dieron dentro de la cárcel. Sintiólo mucho mi padre (buen siglo haya), por ser tal, que robaba a todos las voluntades' (p. 17). 'Un día alabandómela una vieja que me crió, decía que era tal su agrado, que hechizaba a cuantos la trataban; sólo diz que se dijo no sé qué de un cabrón y volar, lo cual la puso cerca de que la diesen plumas con que lo hiciese en público' (p. 17).

12. 'Su oficio fue de barbero; aunque eran tan altos sus pensamientos, que se corría que le llamasen así, diciendo que él era tundidor de mejillas y sastre de barbas' (p. 16).

13. C.B. Morris 'The Unity and Structure of *El buscón: desgracias encadenadas*', Occasional Papers in Modern Languages 1, University of Hull, 1965.

14. 'Aquí hallarás en todo género de picardía – de que pienso que los más gustan – sutilezas, engaños, invenciones y modos, nacidos del ocio, para vivir a la droga, y no poco fruto podrás sacar de él si tienes atención al escarmiento; y, cuando no lo hagas, aprovéchate de los sermones, que dudo nadie compre libro de burlas para apartarse de su natural depravado.' The

sentence 'cuando no lo hagas, aprovéchate de los sermones' can be taken to mean 'if you don't profit from my book's moral lesson, then profit from its sermons'. Since it contains none, this would be a wittier comment on *Guzmán de Alfarache* than interpreting it as a reference to the sermons preached in churches; none the less, it seems to me more natural to take it in this latter sense.

15. E.g. Fernando Lázaro Carreter, 'Originalidad del Buscón' in *Studia Philologica*, Homenaje ofrecido a Dámaso Alonso (Madrid 1961) II, 319–38. I find myself in disagreement with almost everything in this paper. It denies that there is any moral intention in the novel, seeing it as essentially a display of wit behind which there is a cold and impassive vision of a hard world. The author had not read any of the three earlier papers which offered abundant evidence to refute this interpretation: the papers by T.E. May and myself, mentioned below, and P.N. Dunn 'El individuo y la sociedad en *La vida del buscón*', in *Bulletin Hispanique*, LII (1960) 375–96.

16. In what follows I reproduce a substantial section of an early paper of mine, 'The Psychology of the "Pícaro" in "El Buscón" ', in *Modern Language Review*, XLII (1947) 58–69. The validity of my thesis has been accepted by those critics who have read it, but these have been few. Lázaro Carreter, op. cit., did not have access to it; del Monte, op. cit., refers to it but gives the wrong journal, and his treatment of *El buscón* shows no awareness of the existence of my interpretation; neither S. Serrano Poncela 'El buscón, ¿parodia picaresca?', in *Insula*, No. 154 (Sept. 1959) nor Fritz Schalk 'Über Quevedo und *El Buscón*', in *Romanische Forschungen*, LXXIV (1962) 11–30, refer to it, or to May or Dunn, and have really nothing new to say on the novel, repeating the conventional statements about its 'amorality' which have been refuted for the last twenty years. No writer on the picaresque novel in France, England or Germany, as far as I know, has shown any knowledge of my paper. Since my interpretation is cardinal for the revaluation of the Spanish picaresque novel offered in this book, I reproduce the relevant section here, together with the supporting quotations from the text of the novel.

17. 'Todo lo sufría, hasta que un día un muchacho se atrevió a

decirme a voces hijo de una puta hechicera; lo cual, como me lo dijo tan claro–que aún si lo dijera turbio no me pesara–agarré una piedra y descalabréle. Fuime a mi madre corriendo, que me escondiese…Roguéla que me declarase si le podía desmentir con verdad, o me declarase si me había concebido a escote entre muchos, o si era hijo de mi padre sólo. Rióse y dijo: "¡Ah, noramaza! ¿Eso sabes decir? No serás bobo; gracia tienes; muy bien hiciste en quebrarle la cabeza; que esas cosas, aunque sean verdad, no se han de decir." '
(Cap. 11, 24–5).

18. Yo, con esto, quedé como muerto, determinado de coger lo que pudiese en breves días, y salirme de casa de mi padre: tanto pudo conmigo la vergüenza' (ibid.).

19. There is a correspondence between this psychological situation as presented by Quevedo and the findings of the school of Individual Psychology. According to these, the compensation by which the sufferer from an inferiority feeling strives to overcome it never takes the form of actual compensation, but always of over-compensation; the goal of perfection, which is never attainable in practice, becomes the aim, and the possibility of disaster looms large. 'This mechanism of over-compensation in the sphere of unreality, which plunges a man in the depths in direct proportion to the height of his aims for the future, plays a decisive rôle in abnormal development. If the child experiences situations that he interprets in terms of prejudice, oppression and inferiority, the mechanism of over-compensation proportionately raises his future aims to in-ordinate heights…. It is reality that decides whether the goals a man sets before himself are attainable…' (Rudolf Allers *The Psychology of Character*, Engl. trans. [London 1939] 89). Quevedo gives us exactly this situation in the case of Pablos. By setting himself an unattainable goal, he will land in disaster.

20. 'Hubo grandes diferencias entre mis padres sobre a quién había de imitar en el oficio; mas yo, que siempre tuve pensamientos de caballero desde chiquito, nunca me apliqué a uno ni a otro' (Cap. 1, 19).

21. 'Metílos yo en paz, diciendo que quería aprender virtud, resueltamente, e ir con mis buenos pensamientos adelante;

y así, que me pusiese en la escuela, pues sin leer ni escribir no se podía hacer nada' (ibid.).

22. '...recibióme muy alegre; díjome que tenía cara de hombre agudo y de buen entendimiento. Yo con esto, por no desmentirle, di muy bien la lección aquella mañana. Sentábame el maestro junto a sí; ganaba la palmatoria los más días por venir antes, e íbame el postrero por hacer algunos recados de "señora", que así llamábamos la mujer del maestro. Teníalos a todos con semejantes caricias obligados. Favorecíanme demasiado, y con esto creció la envidia de los demás niños' (Cap. II, 22).

23. 'Llegábame a los hijos de los caballeros y personas principales, y particularmente a un hijo de don Alonso Coronel de Zúñiga, con el cual juntaba las meriendas. Íbame a su casa a jugar las fiestas, y acompañábale cada día. Pero los otros, porque no les hablaba, o porque les parecía demasiado punto el mío, siempre andaban poniéndome nombres tocantes al oficio de mi padre' (ibid.).

24. 'En todo esto, siempre me visitaba aquel hijo de don Alonso Coronel de Zúñiga, que se llamaba don Diego; queríame naturalmente, porque trocaba con él los peones, si eran mejores los míos; dábale de lo que almorzaba, y no le pedía de lo que él comía; comprábale estampas, enseñábale a luchar, jugaba con él al toro y entreteníale siempre' (Cap. II, 25).

25. 'Y de paso quiero confesar a v.m. que cuando me empezaron a tirar las berengenas y nabos, que, como yo llevaba plumas en el sombrero, entendí que me habían tenido por mi madre, y que la tiraban, como habían hecho otras veces; y así, como necio y muchacho, dije: "Hermanas, aunque llevo plumas, no soy Aldonza de San Pedro, mi madre", como si ellas no lo echaran de ver por el traje y el rostro. El miedo me disculpa la ignorancia, y el sucederme la desgracia tan de repente' (Cap. II, 29–30).

26. '...determíneme de no volver más a la escuela ni a casa de mis padres...Escribí a mi casa que yo no había menester más ir a la escuela, porque, aunque no sabía bien escribir, para mi intento de ser caballero lo que primero se requería era escribir mal; y que así, yo renunciaba la escuela por no darles gasto, y su casa por ahorrarles pesadumbre' (Cap. II, 31).

27. Here, too, there is a clear parallel with the Adlerian psychologists' analysis of the effects of an ingrained inferiority feeling. See, for example, Rudolf Dreikurs *An Introduction to Individual Psychology* (Eng. trans., London 1935) 29–33.

28. ' "Haz como vieres" dice el refrán, y dice bien. De puro considerar en él, vine a resolverme en ser bellaco con los bellacos, y más que todos, si más pudiese' (Cap. VI, 69).

29. 'Por no ser largo, dejo de contar cómo hacía monte la plaza del pueblo, pues de cajones de tundidores y plateros, y mesas de fruteras–*que nunca se me olvidará la afrenta de cuando fui rey de gallos*–sustentaba la chimenea de casa todo el año' (Cap. VI; 84; italics mine).

30. '...a él le pesaba de dejarme. Díjome que me acomodaría con otro caballero amigo suyo. Yo riyéndome, le dije: "Señor, ya yo soy otro, y otros mis pensamientos, más alto pico y más autoridad me importa tener" ' (Cap. VII; 89–90).

31. 'Iba yo pensando en las muchas dificultades que tenía para profesar honra y virtud, pues había menester tapar primero la poca de mis padres; y luego tener tanta, que me desconociesen por ella; y parecíanme a mí tan bien estos pensamientos honrados, que yo me los agradecía a mí mismo. Decía a solas: "Más se me ha de agradecer a mí, que no he tenido de quién aprender virtud, ni a quién parecer en ella, que al que la heredó de sus abuelos" ' (Cap. IX; 105–6).

32. 'Yo, que vi cuán honrada gente era la que hablaba con mi tío, confieso que me puse colorado, de suerte que no pude disimular la vergüenza...Yo rabiaba ya por comer y por cobrar mi hacienda, y huir de mi tío' (Cap. XI; 135). 'Con estas infamias y vilezas que yo veía, crecíame por instantes el deseo de verme entre gente principal y caballeros' (139). 'Consideraba yo que iba a la corte, donde nadie me conocía–que era la cosa ue más me consolaba' (Cap. XII; 141). '...me importa negar la sangre' (142).

33. A MS version, which is the text published in Clásicos Castellanos, concludes with the promise of a Second Part which will show how he fared worse in America. The novel was, however, printed as being in two parts and the reference to a continuation was dropped. Whatever Quevedo's original intention might have been, the work was published as complete.

34. 'Good and Evil in the *Buscón*', in *The Modern Language Review*, XLV (1950). The section summarized is 331–3. Though this brilliant paper is mentioned by del Monte (who does not seem to have grasped its significance), it appears to have remained unknown to every one else who has dealt with *El buscón*.

35. See Peter N. Dunn *Castillo Solórzano and the Decline of the Spanish Novel* (Oxford 1952).

36. *La vida y hechos de Estebanillo González, hombre de buen amor. Compuesto por él mismo. Dedicada al Excelentísimo Señor Octavio Piccolomini, Duque de Amalfi*...(Antwerp 1646). Angel Valbuena Prat, in his anthology *La novela picaresca* (4th ed. Madrid 1962), includes two works later than this: *Periquillo el de las gallineras* (1668) by Francisco Santos and the autobiography by Diego de Torres Villarroel (1743, 1752, 1758). The former is not, properly speaking, a picaresque novel because it has a saintly hero; the latter is far too remote to form part of the literary movement initiated by *Guzmán de Alfarache*.

4

Germany and the Thirty-Years War

1. See E. R. Moore 'Estebanillo González's Travels in Southern Europe', in *Hispanic Review*, VIII (1940) 24–45; and A. S. Bates 'Historical Characters in Estebanillo González', in *Hispanic Review*, VIII (1940) 63–6. Further reasons for considering the work autobiographical can be found in W. K. Jones 'Estebanillo González', in *Revue Hispanique*, LXXVII (1929) 201–45.
2. 'Díjome el carcelero que me pusiera bien con Dios, sin haberme dado para aquel último trance con qué ponerme bien con Baco' (ed. Clásicos Castellanos, Madrid 1934, I, 226).
   '…despejé el rancho e hincando una rodilla y poniéndome en postura de ballestero, desembuché la talega de culpas, y dejé escueto el almacén de los pecados; y habiendo recibido la bendición y el *ego te absolvo*, quedé tan otro, que sólo sentía el morir, porque juzgaba, según estaba de contrito, que se habían de tocar de su mismo motivo todas las campanas, y alborotarse toda Barcelona, y dejar de ganar su jornal la pobre gente por venirme a ver' (ibid., I, 229–30).
3. The work was published pseudonymously, and with the place of publication disguised, under the title: *Der abenteuerliche Simplicissimus Teutsch. Das ist: Die Beschreibung des Lebens eines seltsamen Vaganten, genannt Melchior Sternfels von Fuchshaim* (Nuremberg 1669). The first English translation, incomplete and in an absurdly and irritatingly archaic style, was that of A. T. S. Goodrick *The Adventurous Simplicissimus* (London 1912), reprinted as *Simplicissimus the Vagabond* in the Broadway Translations (London 1924), and with the original title by the University of Nebraska Press (1962). There are two further incomplete, but better, translations:

The Adventures of a Simpleton by Walter Wallich (New English Library, London 1962), and *Simplicius Simplicissimus* by George Schulz-Behrend (The Library of Liberal Arts, New York 1965). The passages omitted as tedious generally contain the allegorical episodes, which are among the most important. The only complete translation (of the original five Books only) is *Simplicius Simplicissimus* by Hellmuth Weissenborn and Lesley Macdonald (London 1964), which is the one from which I quote. It alters the chapter division of the original, turning the 142 short chapters into 27; this is understandable but is awkward for reference; my notes give the Book and Chapter of the original but the page of this translation. I make some changes in some of the passages I quote from the latter.

4. Manuel García Blanco *Mateo Alemán y la novela picaresca alemana* (Madrid 1928) 17. This is a lecture, not an extensive monograph.

5. Albertinus may have utilized one of the two editions in which Martí's Second Part was published under Alemán's name together with the First Part: Milan 1603 (in one vol. but with different pagination and title-pages), and Brussels 1604 (2 vols.).

6. Both parts were published together under the title *Der Landstörtzer Gusman von Alfarche* [*sic*], *oder Picaro genannt* (Munich 1615).

7. *Der Landstörtzer Gusman von Alfarche, oder Picaro genannt, Dritter Teil* (Frankfurt am Main 1626). For the above account of Alemán's reception and influence in Germany I am indebted to Franz Rauhut 'Influencia de la picaresca española en la literatura alemana', in *Revista de Filología Hispánica*, I (1939) 237–56; Werner Beck, *Die Anfänge des deutschen Schelmenromans. Studien zur frühbarocken Erzählung* (Zürcher Beiträge zur vergleichenden Literaturgeschichte; Zürich 1957); and Edmund Schramm 'Die Einwirkung der spanischen Literatur auf die deutsche', in *Deutsche Philologie im Aufriss*, ed. Wolfgang Stammler (Berlin 1962) II, 147–99.

8. Del Monte, for example, considers Guzmán's conversion inorganic because by implying a 'forced' re-entry into society, after having fallen into an extreme social degradation, it is out

of harmony with the tone of the novel. The only logical end to Guzmán's career, he continues, would have been an 'anti-social asceticism, not a conversion to the religious norm and an adhesion to accepted social standards' (op. cit., 73–4). If by this is meant that Guzmán ought to have become the seventeenth-century equivalent of a Marxist revolutionary, one would suggest that del Monte is prevented by anti-religious prejudice from seeing where his own point leads to, for how can the life of eremitical solitude be considered a re-entry into society and an adhesion to accepted social standards? Francisco Maldonado de Guevara is another critic who does not accept Guzmán's conversion as genuine. He considers that Alemán never wrote a Third Part because it was impossible for him to write one. The novel's basic postulate is that all men are evil, and no conversion can be based on such a postulate since conversion implies some pre-existing virtue ('La teoría de los géneros literarios y la constitución de la novela moderna', in *Estudios dedicados a Menéndez Pidal*, III, 1952, 299–320). This is an odd misreading of the novel.

9. Félix Machado de Silva, Marqués de Montebelo *Tercera Parte de Guzmán de Alfarache...Compuesta por Félix Márquez, Catedrático de Prima en la Picardía, sin salario. Dedícale a la Señoría libre de los magníficos y muy ilustres Señores Esportilleros de Madrid*. This was not published till 1927, in *Revue Hispanique*, LXIX, 1–340, ed. G. Moldenhauer. This narrative provides unintentional light relief when Guzmán is suddenly arrested on his pilgrimage, being mistaken for a previously unknown twin-brother who is the real criminal; this twin is also called Guzmán de Alfarache, has also led a picaresque life and is promptly converted when he hears his brother's story.

10. See J. H. Scholte *Der Simplicissimus und sein Dichter* (Tübingen 1950) 1–14. Rauhut (op. cit., 248) thinks that these allegories were inspired by Quevedo's *Sueños*, in Moscherosch's translation (*c.* 1640).

11. [Bk. I, cap. xv] p. 42. 'In solchen Gedanken entschlief ich vor Unmut und Kälte, mit einem hungerigen Magen, da dünkte mich, gleichwie in einem Traum, als wenn sich alle Bäum, die um meine Wohnung standen, jähling veränderten, und ein ganz ander Ansehen gewönnen, auf jedem Gipfel sass ein

Kavalier, und alle Äst wurden anstatt der Blätter mit allerhand
Kerlen geziert, von solchen hatten etliche lange Spiess, andere
Musketen, kurze Gewehr, Partisanen, Fähnlein, auch
Trommeln und Pfeifen. Dies war lustig anzusehen, weil alles
so ordentlich und fein gradweis sich auseinanderteilete; die
Wurzel aber war von ungültigen Leuten, als Handwerkern,
Taglöhnern, mehrenteils Bauren und dergleichen, welche
nichts destoweniger dem Baum seine Kraft verliehen, und
wider von neuem mitteilten, wenn er solche zuzeiten verlor;
ja sie ersetzten den Mangel der abgefallenen Blätter aus den
ihrigen, zu ihrem eigenen noch grösseren Verderben; benebens
seufzeten sie über diejenigen, so auf dem Baum sassen, und
zwar nicht unbillig, denn die ganze Last des Baums lag auf
ihnen, und drückte sie dermassen, dass ihnen alles Geld aus
den Beuteln, ja hinter sieben Schlössern hervorging; wenn es
aber nicht hervor wollte, so striegelten sie die Commissarii
mit Besen, die man militärische Exekution nannte, dass ihnen
die Seufzer aus dem Herzen, die Tränen aus den Augen, das
Blut aus den Nägeln, und das Mark aus den Beinen herausg-
ging...' I quote from the edition by Alfred Kelletat with
modernized spelling (Dünndruck-Bibliothek der Weltliteratur, Munich 1956) 45.

12. [Bk. II, cap. xxvii] p. 148. '...da sah man, wie die entseelten
Leiber ihres eigenen Gebluts beraubet, und hingegen die
lebendigen mit fremdem Blut beflossen waren' (185).

13. [Bk. II, cap. xxvii] p. 148. '...deren sah man etliche unter
ihren Herrn tot daniederfallen, voller Wunden, welche sie
unverschuldter Weis zu Vergeltung ihrer getreuen Dienste
empfangen hatten; andere fielen um gleicher Ursach willen
auf ihre Reuter, und hatten also in ihrem Tod die Ehr, dass
sie von Denjenigen getragen wurden, welche sie in währendem
Leben tragen müssen; wiederum andere, nachdem sie ihrer
herzhaften Last, die sie kommandiert hatte, entladen worden,
verliessen die Menschen in ihrer Wut und Raserei, rissen aus,
und suchten im weiten Feld ihr erste Freiheit' (184–5).

14. The circular pattern in *Simplicissimus*, from God back to God,
and its roots in mystical literature have been stressed by
Rauhut (op. cit., 245–6, 248).

15. This implied contrast between *simplicitas* and *stultitia* (the

folly that is the way of the world) is made by Paul Gutzwiller *Der Narr bei Grimmelshausen*, Basler Studien zur deutschen Sprache und Literatur No. 20 (Berne 1959). Grimmelshausen's intention is to take his character from *simplicitas*, through *stultitia*, back to *simplicitas*, but according to Gutzwiller this is, in fact, frustrated since, *pace* Grimmelshausen, the last stage is humanly impossible and Simplicissimus is at the end a bigger fool than ever before. This argument will be discussed below.

16. [Bk. IV, cap. xiii] pp. 279–80. 'Wenn ein Reuter sein Pferd, und ein Musketier seine Gesundheit verliert, oder ihm Weib und Kind erkrankt und zurückbleiben will, so ists schon anderthalb Paar Merode-Brüder, ein Gesindlein, so sich mit nichts besser als mit den Zigeunern vergleicht, weil es nicht allein nach seinem Belieben vor, nach, neben und mitten unter der Armee herumstreicht, sondern auch demselben beides an Sitten und Gewohnheit ähnlich ist, da siehet man sie haufen-weis beieinander (wie die Feldhühner im Winter) hinter den Hecken, im Schatten, oder nach ihrer Gelegenheit an der Sonnen, oder irgends um ein Feur herumliegen, Tabak zu saufen und zu faulenzen, wenn unterdessen anderwärts ein rechtschaffener Soldat beim Fähnlein Hitz, Durst, Hunger, Frost und allerhand Elend übersteht. Dort geht eine Schar neben dem Marsch her auf die Mauserei, wenn indessen manch armer Soldat vor Mattigkeit unter seinen Waffen versinken möchte. Sie spolieren vor, neben und hinter der Armee alles was sie antreffen, und was sie nicht geniessen können, verderben sie, also dass die Regimenter, wenn sie in die Quartier oder ins Lager kommen, oft nicht einen guten Trunk Wasser finden, und wenn sie allen Ernstes angehalten werden, bei der Bagage zu bleiben, so wird man oft beinahe dieselbe stärker finden, als die Armee selbst...Ich geschweige hier, wie manches Dorf durch sie sowohl unachtsam- als vorsätzlicherweis verbrannt wird, wie manchen Kerl wie von ihrer eigenen Armee absetzen, plündern, heimlich bestehlen, und wohl gar niedermachen, auch wie mancher Spion sich unter ihnen aufhalten kann, wenn er nämlich nur ein Regiment und Kompagnie aus der Armada zu nennen weiss' (345–6).

17. [Bk. V, cap. i] pp. 312–13. 'Das Land kam mir so fremd vor

gegen andere teutsche Länder, als wenn ich in Brasilia oder in
China gewesen wäre; da sah ich die Leute in dem Frieden
handeln und wandeln, die Ställe standen voll Vieh, die
Baurnhöf liefen voll Hühner, Gäns und Enten, die Strassen
wurden sicher von den Reisenden gebraucht, die Wirtshäuser
sassen voll Leute die sich lustig machten, da war ganz keine
Furcht vor dem Feind, keine Sorg vor der Plünderung, und
keine Angst, sein Gut, Leib noch Leben zu verlieren, ein jeder
lebte sicher unter seinem Weinstock und Feigenbaum, und
zwar gegen andere teutsche Länder zu rechnen in lauter
Wollust und Freud, also dass ich dieses Land für ein irdisch
Paradies hielt, wiewohl es von Art rauh genug zu sein schien'
(391).

18. [Bk. v, cap. xi] p. 338. 'Ich resolvierte mich, weder mehr
nach Ehren noch Geld, noch nach etwas anderm das die Welt
liebt, zu trachten; ja ich nahm mir vor zu philosophieren, und
mich eines gottseligen Lebens zu befleissen, zumalen meine
Unbussfertigkeit zu bereuen, und mich zu erkühnen, gleich
meinem Vater sel. auf die höchsten Staffeln der Tugenden zu
steigen' (426).

19. There is some elucidation (to my mind incomplete and rather
inadequate) of this and later symbolism in the novel in Emil
Ermatinger *Weltdeutung in Grimmelshausens Simplicius
Simplicissimus* (Leipzig and Berlin 1925) 69–87.

20. [Bk. v, cap. xviii] p. 355. '...anstatt dass sie mir darum hätten
dankbar sein sollen, fingen sie an zu lästern, und sagten: Sie
wollten, dass ich mit meinem Saurbrunnen an ein andern Ort
geraten wäre, denn sollte ihre Herrschaft dessen innewerden,
so müsste das ganze Amt Dornstett frönen, und Weg dazu
machen, welches ihnen denn ein grosse Beschwerlichkeit sein
würde. "Hingegen", sagte ich, "habt ihr dessen alle zu
geniessen, eure Hühner, Eier, Butter, Vieh und anders könnt
ihr besser ans Geld bringen." "Nein nein", sagten sie, "nein!
die Herrschaft setzt einen Wirt hin, der wird allein reich, und
wir müssen seine Narren sein, ihm Weg und Steg erhalten,
und werden noch kein Dank dazu davon haben!"..."Ja",
sagten sie, "da wären wir wohl Narren, dass wir uns eine Rut
auf unsern eigenen Hintern machten, wir wollten lieber, dass
dich der Teufel mitsamt deinem Sauerbrunnen holete, du hast

genug gehört, warum wir ihn nicht gerne sehen!" ' (455–7).

21. [Bk. v, cap. xxiii] pp. 370–1. 'Als ich nach meines Vaters seligem Tod in diese Welt kam, da war ich einfältig und rein, aufrecht und redlich, wahrhaftig, demütig, eingezogen, mässig, keusch, schamhaftig, fromm und andächtig; bin aber bald boshaftig, falsch, verlogen, hoffärtig, unruhig, und überall ganz gottlos worden, welche Laster ich alle ohne einen Lehrmeister gelernet' (475).

22. Criticism of this kind is generally misguided as well as trivial. Cf.: 'Simplicius…does not really undergo a transformation of character; he merely alternates between good and evil which are attitudes inherent in him from the start. The "Welt", moreover, is seen as an assembly of fundamentally similar phenomena which the hero encounters successively…. Successive experiences can only confirm the previously known "truth" about the nature of the "world", and show man's freedom to choose in any surroundings either piety or impiety' (H. H. Weil 'The Conception of the Adventurer in German Baroque Literature', in *German Life and Letters*, VI, 1952–3, 290). Indeterminate and repetitive oscillation of this kind is simply not true of *Simplicissimus*: the 'circle' of existence is not a theoretical concept, but an actual movement of experience exemplified by the plot, whereby the particular 'surroundings' in which the 'world' is manifested at any particular point on the 'circle' will influence, though not determine, choice in any particular direction. There is no such thing in the novel as a perfectly balanced (i.e. perfectly 'free') choice between good and evil: at the point that is both the beginning and the end (the solitude of Nature) it is difficult to be impious, the further the protagonist moves away from this point the more difficult it is for him to be pious. Whether one calls this 'transformation of character' or not, there is a moral development marked by clear stages and related all the time to the changing environment.

23. Paul Gutzwiller, op. cit., *passim.*

24. Bertrand Russell 'A Free Man's Worship', in *Mysticism and Logic, and Other Essays* (London 1918) 51–5.

25. K. C. Hayens *Grimmelshausen*, St Andrews University Publication XXXIV (London 1932) 108–9.

26. Edmund Schramm, op. cit., 166.

27. The full title is: *Trutz Simplex: oder Ausführliche und wunderseltsame Lebensbeschreibung der Erzbetrügerin und Landstörtzerin Courasche*, etc. There are two English translations: *Courage, the Adventuress* (published with a translation of *The False Messiah*) by Hans Speier (Princeton, New Jersey 1964); and *The Runagate Courage* by Robert L. Hiller and John C. Osborne (University of Nebraska Press, Lincoln 1965). I quote from the former. The preference for this translation does not imply acceptance of the introductory interpretation of the novel and of Grimmelshausen's ideas in general. The introduction to the second translation is a much safer guide and more interesting.

28. Cap. ix, 124. 'Ich wäre gerne in eine andere Haut geschlüpft, aber beides die Gewohnheit und meine täglichen Gesellschaften wollten mir keine Besserung zulassen, wie denn die allermeisten Leute im Krieg viel eher ärger als frommer zu werden pflegen' (ed. A. Kelletat, Dünndruck-Bibliothek der Weltliteratur, Munich 1958, p. 38). All references to the German text are to this edition.

29. Cap. xxv, 210. 'In Summa, was wollte ich tun? Ich hätte wohl Grössers verdienet, wenn man strenger mit mir hätte prozedieren wollen; aber es war halt im Krieg, und dankte jedermänniglich dem gütigen Himmel (ich sollte gesagt haben "jederweiberlich"), dass die Stadt meiner so taliter qualiter losworden' (110).

30. Cap. xxvii, 216–17. '…und indem ich bei ihnen einen Leutnant antraf, der meiner guten qualitäten und trefflichen Hand zum Stehlen, wie auch etwas Geldes hinter mir wahrnahm samt andern Tugenden, die diese Art Leut gebrauchen, siehe! so wurde ich gleich sein Weib, und hatte diesen Vorteil, dass ich weder Oleum talci noch ander Schmiersel mehr bedurfte, mich weiss und schön zu machen, weil sowohl mein Stand selbst als mein Mann diejenige Couleur von mir erforderte, die man des Teufels Leibfarb nennet. Derowegen fing ich an, mich mit Gänsschmalz, Läussalbe und andern haarfärbenden Unguenten also fleissig zu beschmieren, dass ich in kurzer zeit so höllrieglerisch aussah, als wenn ich mitten in Agypten geboren worden wäre. Ich musste

oft selbst meiner lachen, und mich über meine vielfältige Veränderung verwundern' (115).

31. This is the name of one of Courage's paramours; her translators have rendered it as 'Springinthefield' and 'Hopalong'. The section dealing with Courage in this next novel has been translated as an appendix to *The Runagate Courage*, 187–200.

32. In Bk. v, cap. vi, of his story, Simplicissimus tells, *en passant*, how he paid court to a woman (whom he does not name) until he discovered that she was more interested in fleecing his purse than in marrying him. After he abandons her, she leaves their bastard at his door (cap. ix). Having read his autobiography, Courage is incensed to find herself held up to derision and dishonour. She publishes her own life-story to spite him (hence the title *Trutz Simplex*), to show him what kind of woman he had associated with and to disclose that she had tricked him by fathering on him a child that belonged to neither of them.

33. Of the Spanish *pícaras* the Elena of Salas Barbadillo dies on the gallows; the fate of Justina and the two protagonists in Castillo Solórzano's *Teresa de Manzanares* and *La garduña de Sevilla* is left open (in the sense that it can be either the gallows or repentance) because in each case a Second Part is promised–this could, of course, be a convenient way of shelving indefinitely the literary and moral problem of what to do with one's delinquent in the end.

34. Introduction by Hiller and Osborne to their translation, *The Runagate Courage*, 20.

35. For this transition in the German novel see Arnold Hirsch 'Barockroman und Aufklärungsroman', in *Études Germaniques*, IX (1954) 97–111.

5

The Picaresque Tradition in England and France

1. See F. Rauhut 'Vom Einfluss des spanischen Schelmenromans auf das italienische Schrifttum', in *Romanische Forschungen*, LIV (1940) 382–9.
2. See Joseph Vles *Le Roman picaresque hollandais des XVIIe et XVIIIe siècles et ses modèles espagnols et français* ('sGravenhage 1926).
3. See P. E. Russell 'English Seventeenth-Century Interpretations of Spanish Literature' in *Atlante*, I (1953) 71–3. The whole of this paper is relevant to this chapter.
4. See Dale B. J. Randall *The Golden Tapestry. A Critical Survey of Non-chivalric Spanish Fiction in English Translation, 1543–1657* (Durham, North Carolina, 1963) 170–82.
5. *The Dutch Rogue, or Guzman of Amsterdam* (1683); *Teague O'Dively, or the Irish Rogue* (1690). See Ursula Habel *Die Nachwirkung des picaresken Romans in England (von Nash bis Fielding und Smollett)* (Breslau 1930), 24–32, and Randall, op. cit., 183–4. For the criminal biographies see Frank W. Chandler *The Literature of Roguery* (London, Boston and New York 1907) cap. IV.
6. Chandler, op. cit., 225–6.
7. 'It is absolutely original as an attempt at realistic fiction' (Edmund Gosse *A History of Eighteenth Century Literature*, London 1889, 85); '...it is scarcely an exaggeration to call it the first modern English novel' (G. B. Harrison, Introduction to Everyman's Library edition, 1928); 'Der realistische Charakter des kleinen Werkes kann nicht genug betont werden, und man kann mit Recht behaupten, dass wir...

geradezu einen Vorläufer des realistischen Romans späterer
Zeiten vor uns haben' (Wolfgang Sachs *Der typisch
puritanische Ideengehalt in Bunyan's Life and Death of
Mr. Badman*, Leipzig Dissertation, 1936, 19); '...in order
that it might reach a wide public [Bunyan] employed the
technique of fictitious memoir... *Mr. Badman* is an important
picture of town life, but it is more important in the development
of the novel (to Defoe's villain-heroes and to *Jonathan Wild*)
than as a social document' (Maurice Hussy 'Bunyan's "The
Life and Death of Mr. Badman" ', in *Congregational
Quarterly*, XXVIII [1950] 359, 366).

8. E. A. Baker *The History of the English Novel* (London 1929)
   III, 69.
9. '*Wiseman*...from a child he was very bad; his very beginning
   was ominous, and presaged that no good end was, in likelihood,
   to follow thereupon. There were several sins that he was given
   to, when but a little one, that manifested him to be notoriously
   infected with original corruption; for I dare say he learned
   none of them of his father and mother; nor was he admitted
   to go much abroad among other children that were vile, to
   learn to sin of them....

   '*Attentive*. This was a bad beginning indeed, and did
   demonstrate that he was, as you say, polluted, very much
   polluted with original corruption. For to speak my mind
   freely, I do confess that it is mine opinion that children come
   polluted with sin into the world, and that ofttimes the sins of
   their youth, especially while they are very young, are rather
   by virtue of indwelling sin, than by examples that are set
   before them by others.' (*Mr. Badman*, Everyman's Library,
   London and New York 1963, 153).
10. See, e.g., Bonamy Dobrée 'Some Aspects of Defoe's Prose',
    in *Pope and his Contemporaries, Essays presented to
    George Sherburn*, ed. Clifford and Landa (Oxford 1949).
11. Ian Watt *The Rise of the Novel* (Penguin Books 1963) 132.
12. Cf. 'This is Defoe's strength, that he is able to extricate himself
    as an artist from conventional morality (even in the very act
    of paying lip-service to it) and to concentrate on the surface-
    texture of life. And his limitation is that he has no other
    morality to put in its place. That is why his books, except

perhaps *Robinson Crusoe* and *Roxana*, are ultimately without pattern. For the mere presentation of a man's life is not pattern enough, and the assumption that surface-texture is in the end an alternative to, or indeed separable from, point of view is an illusion' (Arnold Kettle *An Introduction to the English Novel*, Arrow Books 1962, I, 66).

13. See Maximillian E. Novak *Defoe and the Nature of Man* (Oxford 1963).

14. J. R. Moore *Daniel Defoe, Citizen of the Modern World* (Chicago 1958) 242.

15. I quote from the edition by George A. Aitken, 2 vols. (London 1895) I, xvi.

16. E.g. Pierre Jobit 'L'Espagne et la littérature française au XVIIᵉ siècle français', in G. Grente *Dictionnaire des Lettres Françaises, Le dix-septième siècle* (Paris 1944) 398–404, devotes a whole column to the influence of Cervantes and only four lines to the existence of a Spanish picaresque novel. This is dealt with in the volume on the eighteenth century only in connexion with Lesage, although the latter's treatment of picaresque material can only be explained through the seventeenth-century translations of the Spanish works.

17. Angel Valbuena Prat calls these works the 'current of a French picaresque' (*La novela picaresca española*, Aguilar, Madrid 1962, 113–14.) See also Paul Verdevoye 'La novela picaresca en Francia', in *Clavileño*, No. 35 (1955) 32.

18. For information about these translations I am indebted to Rolf Greifelt 'Die französischen Übersetzungen des spanischen Schelmenromans im 17. Jahrhundert', in *Romanische Forschungen*, L (1936) 51–84. For bibliographical details see Frank W. Chandler 'A Bibliography of Spanish Romances of Roguery, 1554–1668, and their Translations', in *Romances of Roguery* (New York and London 1899) 399 ff.

19. 'Les espagnols ont quelque chose dessus nous en l'ordre et en l'invention d'une histoire... mais en contrechange ils sont bien éloignés aussi de la pureté de nos écrits.' I have not seen this translation or *les Relations morales* of Bishop Camus mentioned below. I am indebted for both quotations to Greifelt, 70, 80.

20. I have not seen the first edition, and quote from the Rouen 1646 edition of both Parts.

21. 'Les Romans Comiques ou Satyriques nous semblent plutôt des images de l'histoire que tous les autres; les actions communes de la vie étant leur objet, il est plus facile d'y rencontrer de la vérité.' 'Les espagnols sont les premiers qui ont fait des romans vraisemblables et divertissants…*le Guzman d'Alfarache* ne décrit pas seulement la vie des gueux et des voleurs: beaucoup de gens de condition y trouvent leur peinture avec des avertissements pour se reformer à l'avenir. Il est vrai qu'on y a repris les discours de morale qui semblent trop longs pour cette sorte de livres. *L'Écuyer de Marc d'Obregon* tombe encore dans cette faute, et même il a moins d'aventures plaisantes. *Lazarillo de Tormes* est plus gaillard, et *le Buscon* aussi, dont l'un est un valet d'aveugle et l'autre un voleur et un fripon. Nous les accouplerons à *la Narquoise Justine* et à *la Fouine de Séville*, qui sont des femmes de belle humeur dont on a écrit les actions…Je nomme des livres qui sont espagnols d'origine, mais qui ayant été faits français par la traduction, peuvent tenir leur rang en ce lieu.' (*La Bibliothèque française, de M.C. Sorel. Ou le choix et l'examen des livres français* (Paris 1664) 169, 172–3.

22. 'Et comme sa louable fin est le profit commun, aussi moralise-t-il sur chaque chose de dessein formé; mais avec si peu d'égard et de suite, qu'il n'y a si bon pied qui le suive trois lignes sans le perdre. Vous n'y voyez ni rapport ni distinction, ni liaison ni période: et quoique tout ce qu'il dit soit bon, la façon dont il le dit ne peut être que mauvaise.'

23. I have not seen any edition earlier than the eighth, Amsterdam 1728. The translator was first identified as Gabriel Bremond. According to the British Museum catalogue this is incorrect.

24. The earliest edition I have seen is the fifth, Maestricht 1777.

25. Léo Claretie *Lesage romancier* (Paris 1890) 178.

26. Charles Dédéyan, giving a synopsis of *Guzmán*, writes: 'Hélas, la félicité ne dure pas et le roman finit tristement par sa con-damnation aux galères' (*Lesage et Gil Blas*, Paris 1965, 1, 62).

27. *The Life of Guzman d'Alfarache, or the Spanish Rogue. Done into English, from the New French Version and compared with the Original. By several hands* (London 1707).

28. The first edition: *The Life and Adventures of Guzman d'Alfarache or The Spanish Rogue. Translated from the excellent French edition by Mons. Le Sage. By John Henry Brady.* London 1821. Alemán is given as the author in the preface. The 1881 edition: *The Life and Adventures of Lazarillo de Tormes. Translated from the Spanish of Don Diego Hurtado de Mendoza by Thomas Roscoe.*/*The Life and Adventures of Guzman d'Alfarache by Mateo Aleman from the French edition of Le Sage. By John Henry Brady* (London 1881).

29. The British Museum copy, which is the only one I have seen, has a separate title page: *L'Aventurier Buscon, histoire divertissante... À Bruxelles, Chez Josse de Grieck* 1700 but comprises pp. 239–497 of vol. 1 of *Les Oeuvres de Don Francisco de Quevedo Villegas...Nouvelle traduction de l'espagnol en français par le Sr. Raclots parisien...A Bruxelles, Chez Josse de Grieck* 1699.

30. 'Seulement vous dirai-je en passant, qu'elle a été façonnée à la française d'une main qui l'a merveilleusement bien embellie; comme il sera facilement reconnu de ceux qui sont capable de juger de tels ouvrages' (*L'Aventurier Buscon, histoire facétieuse ...à Paris* 1633). This preface by the printer states that the translator is Monsieur de la Geneste, translator of Quevedo's *Sueños*.

31. Chandler *Romances of Roguery*, 451–2; Greifelt, op. cit., 76–7; Verdevoye, op. cit., 31–2.

32. From p. 204, line 13 onwards, of the Clásicos Castellanos edition of 1960.

33. It stops at p. 246, line 24, of the above edition.

34. Henry Thomas 'The English Translations of Quevedo's *La Vida del Buscón*', in *Revue Hispanique*, LXXXI (1933) 283–5. Thomas summarizes La Geneste's new ending but makes no mention of the crucial omissions.

35. 'Je m'attendais donc à passer le pas; néanmoins mon attente fut trompée. Mes docteurs m'ayant abandonné, et laissé le champ libre à la nature, me sauvèrent par ce moyen. La fièvre, qui selon leur pronostic devait m'emporter, me quitta comme pour leur en donner le démenti. Je me rétablis peu à peu, par le plus grand bonheur du monde: une parfaite tranquillité d'esprit devint le fruit de ma maladie. Je n'eus

point alors besoin d'être consolé. Je gardai pour les richesses
et pour les honneurs tout le mépris que l'opinion d'une mort
prochaine m'en avait fait concevoir; et, rendu à moi-même,
je bénis mon malheur. J'en remerciai le ciel comme d'une
grâce particulière qu'il m'avait faite; et je pris une ferme
résolution de ne plus retourner à la cour, quand le duc de
Lerme voudrait m'y rappeler. Je me proposai plutôt, si jamais
je sortais de prison, d'acheter une chaumière, et d'y aller vivre
en philosophe' (Book IX, cap. viii).

36. Sometimes the wit is neatly pointed (' "Venez, ma nièce",
    lui dit sa mère', Book XII, cap. i); more often it is, for our
    modern taste, rather flat (the bandits say of the servants of
    the law: 'ils sont plus humains que nous: car souvent nous
    ôtons la vie aux innocents, et eux quelquefois la sauvent même
    aux coupables', Book I, cap. v); sometimes it palls by
    repetition, like the joke about doctors not curing their
    patients, which is made every time they appear, and that is not
    seldom.

37. Vivienne Mylne 'Structure and Symbolism in *Gil Blas*', in
    French Studies, XV (1961) 134–45. This is an admirable paper.

38. N. Wagner 'Quelques cadres d'étude pour "Gil Blas" ', in
    L'Information littéraire, VIII (1956) 38b. All that this article
    succeeds in showing is that Lesage possesses a certain skill in
    constructing a long and coherent narrative out of an episodic
    plot. This does not give it a pattern of significance.

39. Jürgen von Stackelberg 'Die "Moral" des *Gil Blas* (Lesage
    und die Moralistik)', in *Romanische Forschungen*, LXXIV
    (1962) 357–8. The moral that wealth corrupts is attributed to
    Tacitus and traced through Guicciardini to La Rochefoucauld
    –as if it were not a commonplace of the Stoic-Christian
    tradition.

40. Von Stackelberg op. cit., 351–2.

41. Charles Duff, the translator of Quevedo, in a letter to the
    author, quoted in L. Melville *The Life and Letters of
    Tobias Smollett* (London 1926) 120.

42. For a comparison of the two novels see Alexandre Lawrence
    'L'Influence de Lesage sur Smollett', in *Revue de Littérature
    Comparée*, XII (1932) 533–45.

43. Compare the *Cambridge History of English Literature*, X (1952).

45: 'The picaresque novel in general, which burst into activity soon after the publication of *Roderick Random*, was under heavy obligations to Smollett, and nowhere more so than in its first modern example, *Pickwick*.'

44. F. McCombie 'Count Fathom and *El Buscón*', in *Notes and Queries*, CCV (1960) 297–9. The author is unaware that he is comparing *Count Fathom* not with the real *Buscón* but with La Geneste's version, which naturally invalidates some of his conclusions.

45. David Hume *Enquiries concerning the Human Understanding and concerning the Principles of Morals*, ed. L. A. Selby-Bigge (Oxford 1902) 268, 270.

46. Basil Willey *The Eighteenth Century Background* (London 1950) 123.

47. Nigel Walker *Crime and Punishment: the Penal System in Theory, Law and Practice in Britain* (Edinburgh 1965) 91.

48. Op. cit., 144–5.

INDEX

INDEX